John Newcombe was born in Sydney, Australia, in 1944. He won the Wimbledon singles championship in 1967, 1970 and 1971, and the doubles in 1965, 1966, 1968, 1969 and 1970. He is currently running a tennis ranch.

JOHN
NEWCOMBE
BEDSIDE
TENNIS

Illustrations by Stan McMurtry
Fontana/Collins

First published in Great Britain
by Elm Tree Books Ltd 1983
First issued in Fontana Paperbacks 1984

Editor Michael Leitch
Designed by David Pocknell's Company Ltd
Production Reynolds Clark Associates Ltd

Made by Lennard Books, Mackerye End
Harpenden, Herts AL5 5DR

Printed and bound in Great Britain by
William Collins Sons & Co. Ltd, Glasgow

CONTENTS

The Wall and the Street. Those were the arenas where the dream took shape. Hoad and Rosewall had just hit the top at international level; shortly before them Sedgman and McGregor, and before them Adrian Quist and John Bromwich, had begun a dynasty which meant that by the Fifties Australia had a big stock of kids who were fired by the idea of becoming tennis champions.

From the age of seven I had been having a lesson one hour a week, and over the next three years a routine developed. I'd play matches all day Saturday and Sunday, and have a practice session one day a week with one of the other young players. The rest of the time, I'd come home after school and go out to the wall.

I had a net marked out in chalk with targets across the top of the net. From the wall I'd measured out the place where the baseline should be, and from there I'd practise serving at the targets on the wall, maybe for forty minutes at a time. Another game was to stand close to the wall and practise quick-volleying, trying to beat the wall. Or I'd stand on the

baseline and toss the ball up in the air, practising my service action until the ball was landing pat each time on the same spot in front of me.

At other times I'd go and hit a ball around in the street with some of the boys who lived in my area. One boy in particular, called David Bogg, played fairly well. He was five or six years older than me and we had some pretty fierce contests.

All very commendable, you might think. Nothing wrong with that. That's what I thought, too, until a couple of years ago I made an appearance on an Australian TV comedy show hosted by Paul Hogan. By then I was the established tennis star, scheduled for the interview spot, or that's what they told me before we started. After the usual introduction, I came on and began chatting with Paul in front of a studio audience. It was all straight tennis stuff to begin with, then he said:

'Now we've got a little item from your past, John. We've got this guy you used to hit with on the street at home.'

'Oh,' I said, and while I was still trying to figure out how they'd done a 'This Is Your Life' on me, and whether I was altogether happy about it, a voice came out from behind a screen:

'John, do you remember those times we used to hit balls out on the street each evening?'

Paul said: 'Do you know who that is?'

'Yee-ees,' I was saying, when out came this unmistakeable figure. 'Oh, hello David!' I said, still fairly amazed by it all but glad to see David Bogg again. He joined us and we reminisced about the old times for a couple of minutes. Then Paul said:

'Now, John, there's someone else you used to know. Just listen a second, will you?'

The next voice from behind the screen was softer, alluring, mysterious – and female too!

'John,' she murmured, 'do you remember how we used to go parking down at the Oval in your Volkswagen? Do you remember the things we used to do? I've never forgotten those terrific evenings, John.'

The studio lights seemed suddenly hotter. The facts were embarrassingly close to the mark, and already I was thinking of one particular girl. But we were on National Television, and there was no way I wanted to say her name – even if I could remember it! My thoughts in the next moments were mainly on the lines of 'How am I going to get out of this hole?!' The studio audience were warming to the spectacle of my obvious discomfort... when out she came!

'Hello, John!' she cried, with a radiant smile. 'Isn't this just great?'

We faced each other. Now I was in an even worse predicament. No-one would have denied that she was an attractive girl. What's more, she'd named the venue, the car was right, and everything might have fallen into place but for the one disturbing detail that she wasn't the girl I'd been thinking of. In fact, I didn't *think* I'd ever seen her before! But how could I say that? How could I say anything?

'John . . . John, you do remember me, don't you?'

The girl by now was beginning to register distress at my total lack of response.

'But John. It's *Me*. You *know...*'

As I fought with my shocked brain to produce an answer, her features began juddering slightly in that terrible pause before tears bulge out and total breakdown takes over. I remained mute, and waited for the storm to break.

'I've never been so . . .' she was whimpering before long. 'I mean, this is the most humiliating moment of . . .'

At that moment angry shouting could be heard from the direction of the audience; loud enough to make all heads turn. 'Hey listen! Let me out. Let me out will you!' A huge guy had climbed out of his seat, reached the nearest aisle and was thudding down the steps to the studio floor. I just had time to stand up before he stuck his great face somewhere over my nose.

'Listen, Newcombe! What the hell are you playing at with my fiancée? You've given her the most embarrassing time of her life! Who d'ya think you are, anyway? Who the *hell* do you think you are?'

Then he wheeled on Paul Hogan.

TONIGHT!

THE
PAUL
HOGAN
COMEDY
SHOW

A LAUGH A MINUTE!

6

'Yeah! And if there's anyone to blame apart from him, it's you! You arranged this whole thing. I'm gonna fix *you* up so you never . . .'

Paul's response was to move in close to the big man. I hardly saw his fist move it was so fast. WHOOOMPH! Hogan ripped the guy in the stomach and felled him right there on the studio floor. As the fiancé crumpled up, clutching at his busted gut, Hogan shouted off-stage: 'Get him outa here!' Then he turned and gestured me back to my chair. He sat down:

'Now, John,' he said, crossing one leg over the other, as though nothing at all out of the ordinary had happened, 'about the Davis Cup. Can we switch to that?'

Only after about another twenty seconds did it fully come home to me that I'd been set up! Later, I saw close-ups of my face during the whole fiasco, which they had been shooting from a specially positioned camera. It wasn't a pretty sight. Have you ever seen a Haunted Tennis Player?

There are quite a few players who get fervently attached to a particular pair of shorts. After each match they wash them out and wear them the next day. In time the shorts begin to show their age and have to be darned and patched. Even when they turn grey-green with mould and develop the textile equivalent of metal fatigue, the player only discards them when he reaches the stage of risking arrest for indecency if he keeps them any longer. He may not admit he is being superstitious, but he is.

There are players who react to tense moments on court by refusing to cross a white line when they change ends. Vitas Gerulaitis is one such. He will walk outside the side-line and across the back of the court rather than step over a line. The late Rafael Osuna was another. Whenever he changed ends he would only cross a line where it intersected with another – even if this added another twenty feet to his journey.

There are players whose pre-service routine of bouncing the ball three or four times extends with the approach of set point to an agonized juggling act of fourteen or fifteen bounces. With Andres Gimeno it seemed he sometimes just didn't want to serve at all, and gladly would have delayed the fatal moment until nightfall . . . or maybe until his opponent went giddy from watching and waiting.

There was once a small boy in Sydney, Australia, who had a peaked cap. This boy liked his peaked cap and wore it from the day he started out in competitive tennis. He liked his peaked cap so much that he wouldn't leave home for a match without first checking to make sure the cap was in his tennis bag. He was a very promising young tennis

player, and won many more matches than he lost. He saw the cap, not surprisingly, as a 'lucky' cap. It wasn't like a racket, or a pair of shorts, in that he didn't *have* to have it, but as long as he *did* have it he kept winning matches.

One day, when he was thirteen, he set out to play in the final of a state competition. As usual he checked to make sure the cap was in his tennis bag before he left home. He reached the ground, changed, and went to watch one of the early matches. While he was out of the dressing-room, someone came along and took the peaked cap. When the boy came back and found the cap was gone, all hell broke loose inside his head. He knew at once the cap had been stolen and he wasn't going to get it back in time for his match. Perhaps, he thought, I shouldn't play the match. I haven't got much hope of winning now.

Fortunately, a grown-up came along at that moment and knocked some sense into him. Still nagged by self-doubt, and grieving for his cap, the boy eventually went out on the court. For a time, it did seem as if the loss of the cap had seriously undermined his game. Gradually, though, he fought against his nerves, got into the match . . . and won it!

I tell that touching little story because for me it brought two happy endings. (Did you guess it was me, by the way? You did? Terrific!) Anyway, the first happy ending was simply that I'd won the match without the lucky peaked cap. The second was more far-reaching, because that experience cured me forever of getting hooked on superstitions, which, in a full career of serious tennis, must be worth more than just a few points.

Lindo's law

That I was able to drag myself out of instant despair after losing my peaked cap, and win, was certainly a tribute to the efforts of my coach, Henry Lindo. He insisted that the young players he coached should acquire a sound temperament. This meant learning not to show dismay on the court, whatever the player might feel inside. It was okay to joke a bit – provided you didn't lose your concentration – but if you registered dismay or frustration, all you did was to encourage your opponent.

This seemed logical at the time, and it has served me well over the years as a guiding principle. Approaches to the game vary, though, and lately temperament has become a much more active ingredient, and one that some of the more volatile players exploit on court to obtain an advantage (see also 'The Name of the Game', below).

The Fifties were more straightforward times than the Eighties, and a young player starting out today could expect a very different tennis education from my own. For one thing, he or she would be taking organized lessons much earlier in life; for another, the practice sessions would be longer and physically harder.

To illustrate the difference in approach, let me tell you that I was all of seven years old before my parents took me along to the Saturday morning tennis school. They had watched me play since I was about five and a half, so they had some idea of what I could do. But to the people at the tennis school I was just some kid – and apparently pretty young, too. In fact, that was their first concern. After looking at me for about 0.5 seconds, they turned to my parents and said:

'How old is he?'

'He's seven.'

'Oh, sorry,' came the instant reply. 'We don't take anyone until they're ten years of age.'

Fortunately, my parents got round this difficulty by asking if one of the coaches would mind having a look at me to see how I played. They agreed, and I evidently hit the ball well enough because they then said they'd take me on. Today, a kid who hasn't got started by the age of eight, let alone ten, would be regarded as dangerously close to being over the hill.

Which system is better, the old or the new? There is no easy answer, but sometimes I feel it's getting like the arms race, and that the main reason for today's intensive coaching is that, in tennis schools in other parts of the country, and in other continents too, other promising kids are being trained equally hard, if not harder. So, when they all eventually meet in competition, how can you expect your kid to win if he or she hasn't had a sufficiently tough training?

That, whether you approve of it or not, is how the argument seems to run. Maybe it's time all the coaches agreed to relax a little. I couldn't see it lasting, though. 'Hey, wait a minute,' someone would soon be saying. 'You want *your* kid to lose?'

Thirty years ago the Accomplished Tennis Player (male) wore a baggy pair of shorts and had one, possibly two shirts. The shirts of *really* accomplished players had holes under the armpits which emphasized the status and heavy fixture-list of the wearer, like campaign medals. Shirts were never ironed during the season. At this upper level of the game, players had two rackets, and the best thing you could say about these battered weapons of war was that they were well worn-in, or that the player felt 'comfortable' with them.

Even if not everyone with holes under the armpits was a true 'tennis bum',* it was the image that nearly all male tennis players managed to convey until well into the Sixties. An essential factor in keeping alive this 'rugged-but-drab' look was colour. Provided, of course, that it was white. Other sports may have embraced different colours since the 19th century, but until the late 1960s tennis retained a monastic fidelity to white.

Then came the big switch, launched in 1968 when the first 'heavyweight' professional circuits got under way. These were World Championship Tennis (WCT), and the National Tennis League. I was one of the new WCT pros, and straight away the organizers decided that white was right no longer. It came as something of a shock to realize that we would have to abandon our traditional outfits and get into coloured clothing. It wasn't simply personal prejudice, there were practical difficulties too. To begin with, coloured clothing simply wasn't available from the companies that manufactured tennis gear.

We ended up at the local stores, raking over mound after mound of 'sports' clothing in search of something passable. The result was that I made my first professional appearance in a pair of tan shorts, a

* True tennis bums belonged to a post-war band of roving amateur mercenaries, who travelled the world and just about scraped by on whatever expenses and perks they could drum up from local associations.

lemon-green shirt, white socks and white shoes. As I ran on court Tony Roche, deciding I'd turned into some overgrown kid who'd lost his way to the beach, unkindly said: 'Where's your lollipop?'

The making of pink

Revolution it may have been, but it was many years before the clothing manufacturers were designing the kind of well-coordinated outfits, with neat trims and so on, that you see everywhere today. So slow was the transition, as late as 1974 I still felt highly self-conscious about pulling on a pink shirt.

I had just signed my first important contract with a clothing manufacturer, and they wanted me to wear a pink shirt they had just produced. From the beginning of that year, and for the next four months, I was to wear pink at every match. The début of the shirt was scheduled for an indoor match in New York, and at that stage just the sight of it in my bag, all pale and resolutely non-macho, made me distinctly nervous. When the time came to wear it, I slipped into a corner of the dressing-room as a way of curtailing as far as possible the pre-match derision of the other guys. There was some, of course; they were just as startled as I was when they first saw it. But in general things were remarkably quiet on the insults front. Out on court, the prospects seemed good. I was playing well, and by the middle of the year was No 1 in the world. It was the making of pink. The shirt became the big seller that the manufacturer had predicted, and in the dressing-room I no longer felt the need to fumble around in the shadows.

If there was a drawback to the new coloured outfits, it was that you needed a bag twice the size to carry all the extra stuff. Before, when I left Australia for a six-month tour, I had needed six tennis shirts, four pairs of shorts, six jockstraps, six pairs of socks, two pairs of shoes and some white sweatbands. All of a sudden there was this explosion in the tennis wardrobe, and people had to 'think coordinated'. The wristbands you wore couldn't be just the next pair in the bag. They had to have the right trim to match the socks that went with the shorts that went with the shirt, etc. If you were into headbands as well, that was another thing that could go wrong.

Mercifully, perhaps, brightly coloured outfits were really popular for only a season or two, and now things are a lot quieter, with most of the players back to wearing whites with a coloured trim. The clothing manufacturers still do well out of it, and the players are still happy to be under contract to them. Recently there has been a move towards stripes, and they may catch on more. Meanwhile the field is wide open if some young Mr Rainbow wants to come in and start setting a new trend towards bright colours – provided he is a good tennis player too! But nowadays what the sponsors look for is somewhere to fix their player's logo. The logo has become more important than the clothing, and for the very good reason that it can be applied to a range of other items that a successful player might be asked to sponsor. All of which leads us to . . .

I was sitting in a restaurant in Sydney with my wife and some friends when this lady, a total stranger, came up to my table. She didn't say anything, just bent forward, took a grip on my moustache, and gave it a sharp tug.

'Aaah!' she cried.

I thought it was me that should have been doing the yelling. What was going on anyway?

'Aaah!' she cried again, and gave my moustache another tug. As I looked up at her through watering eyes she added, by way of triumphant explanation:

'You *haven't* shaved it off!'

Then I remembered the commercial.

WAITER. THERE'S A MOUSTACHE IN MY SOUP

I guess a lot of people with moustaches get them pulled once in a while. My problem is that my moustache isn't just a moustache: it's a logo as well, and that's a much more serious area. It's part of what the advertising people call my Recognition Factor, and as such is not to be tampered with. In case this is beginning to sound obscure, I will try to explain.

I first grew my moustache back in 1970, liked it, and decided to keep it. On the tennis circuit, people grew accustomed to it, and then in 1974 it became just about indispensable. That was the year I signed with a clothing manufacturer, and they decided I should have a personal logo. Their advertising agents produced several designs, and one day in New York I went to an office to help make the final choice. My agents were there as well, plus the clothing manufacturer and their advertising people. The room was fast filling up with experts. Then someone came in with an armful of rough designs and scattered them all over the floor. The one you see below came out the winner, and that's how the moustache and I became business partners.

Largest, Heaviest, Longest, Widest . . .

Fortunately, the logo has worked well as a marketing device, and I've been able to use it in several ways. Down at my tennis ranch in Texas, for instance, we now have what we claim is the world's largest moustache. There are four indoor courts at the ranch, all under one roof. Someone had the bright idea of giving the ranch some aerial publicity, so we got up on the roof and graphed out the moustache across the whole span, and then painted it in. If, one day, you are in the air over New Braunfels, see if you can find it. We've also submitted a photo to the *Guinness Book of Records* but they haven't put it in the book yet – even though it's more than a hundred feet longer than the current titleholder. Didn't you get the photo, Guinness?

One night in a Persian bathroom . . .

In our life together, I would say I have been 99 per cent faithful to my moustache. Which is another way of saying it's only been off once. That was after a lively night in Tehran (before the Islamic Revolution, when you could get a beer without going to gaol and collecting sixty lashes). I was with a group of tennis players and we had met up with a BOAC crew staying at the same hotel. We were up in someone's room having a couple of drinks, when one of the airline people started needling me about my moustache, how essential it must be to my image, did I have it insured, and so forth. Perhaps they put something in my beer as well, because I started saying:

'Listen, I can shave the bloody thing off if I want to.'

'No you can't,' they said.

'What do you mean, I can't?'

'Of course you can't. You're stuck with it for the rest of your days.'

In the bathroom I found one of those twin-headed electric shavers. Five minutes later my moustache lay ripped and shredded in the wash-basin. Next morning, I woke up and found this huge rash across the top of my lip. Sanity returned with a jolt, and I spent the next three days trying to contact my wife in Hamburg to explain to her what had happened before she saw for herself and jumped to her own conclusions. The Persian telephone service wasn't equal to the task, however, so when she arrived at Hamburg airport to meet me, she found herself facing the Mauve Monster, a strange and hideous creature notable for his embarrassed grin and total inability to sound convincing whenever he spoke.

Later, I think my wife accepted that the incident had been as innocent as it was ridiculous. At the airport, though, anything I said sounded far *too* innocent to be believed.

Cut! Cut! Cut!

The next time my wife saw me without my moustache, there was no threat to marital harmony. What happened was, Wilkinson Sword wanted me to do a razor advertisement for television. The script was deceptively simple: I shaved off my moustache. Or did I?

As the film begins, there I am shaving away with my Wilkinson Sword razor. It's giving me such a terrific shave that I get carried away, so when I have finished shaving the usual bits I go on and attack my moustache. Whoosh! Slice it off. (So far so good, except that in the last part of the sequence, as I come down through the moustache, the viewer does not see that there is no blade in the razor.)

The scene then cuts to an actor with a moustache similar to my own, and he is filmed in close-up shaving off the whole thing. Cut to a pair of hands picking up a replica of my moustache from a wash-basin. Cut to me, looking as if I have just finished sticking the replica into position. In the final shot I look into the camera, wink, and say: 'But I wouldn't want to disappoint my fans.'

Cut, in real life, to a restaurant in Sydney, one month after we'd made the commercial. A lady is coming up to my table. She doesn't say anything, just bends forward and takes a grip on my . . . 'Aaaah!'

There is a creeping sickness in the modern game. Some commentators politely refer to it as putting pressure on an opponent. I think you need also to distinguish between lawful aggression and those dubious practices for which a better word is intimidation. Intimidation of opponents, intimidation of line judges, intimidation of umpires and referees.

Why do the players who pull these dubious tricks seem to think that success can only be gained if the snarl on their face is fiercer than the other guy's? The source of this disturbing and disturbed outlook seems to lie in the minds of players for whom tennis has ceased to be a sport.

They have developed an accountant's mentality towards the game. Their lives are ruled by business considerations and their play is haunted by equations founded on dollars per point, per game, per set, per match, per tournament, per year (per *financial* year, that is). In the process, their love of the game can be all but destroyed. They no longer seek ways to put something back into the game which made them wealthy and famous. They prefer to handle their affairs as individuals, and let the game run itself. The players' association does not interest them as a means of enforcing change. They tend to make extravagant solo gestures, such as refusing to compete at a major tournament. But with each petty rebellion they tarnish the common cause, which must be to create better playing conditions for *all* competitors.

Who are they, these groaners and whingers? It is no great problem to name *some* names, but there are at least two drawbacks to doing this. First, people change their views all the time, and there is a risk of being unfair to someone who is recovering his or her true appetite

20

for the game. Second, by naming some of the guilty – those you are sure about – you risk letting others off the hook who may be just as guilty but whom you have excluded from your list because you are not quite sure and wish to give them the benefit of the doubt.

In the first category, and for the best of reasons, I would definitely put Jimmy Connors. It is one of the most heartening signs for the future of tennis that Jimmy has shaken off the attitudes that made him the villain of the piece, the brash, arrogant figure, all grunt and no grin, forever arguing with himself, the crowd, the match officials – the man that fewer and fewer fans of tennis wanted to see win his matches. In the last three years Jimmy has changed around completely. He relates much better to the crowd, and his game has improved at that very point when he seemed to have nowhere else to go but down. Put simply, he is enjoying his tennis again. This has not stopped him wanting to win just as much as ever, but he seems to have realized that he gets more out of his tennis if he enjoys himself at the same time. He has rediscovered what might have been self-evident (but evidently was not), namely that it is much more fun to have the crowd with him than against him, and that, contrary to the words of the whingers' motto, it is *not* necessary to 'hate to be great'. So, re-enter Jimmy Connors, 'People's Champion', with that quirky little grin securely back in place.

On the other side of the hate-to-be-great syndrome is John McEnroe. For some while he has found himself in the trap of thinking he cannot win unless he finds something or someone to blow up at. The longer he goes on in that state of mind the worse it may be for him. He is burning up reserves of mental and emotional energy at such a rate that he is in danger of burning out altogether, long before his time. What he needs is a dose of the elation that has fired up the new Connors. I just hope he finds some soon. At Wimbledon in 1982 we saw some promising signs – he made peace with the Committee, was awarded the membership denied him in 1981, and took part in a rousing but encouragingly good-tempered singles final with Jimmy Connors. McEnroe in fact strengthened his standing at Wimbledon in a year when several eminent players failed to turn up for 'personal' reasons, some of which to my mind bordered dangerously on the self-indulgent.

The opponent's dilemma

In 1981 McEnroe provided the Wimbledon crowd with some vintage examples of those dubious practices I mentioned earlier. In his semi-final singles against Rod Frawley, he queried no less than thirteen line calls. This meant that for thirteen separate periods of the match McEnroe was busy charging up his ego by yelling at the line judges and the umpire – while Frawley was left out in the cold with nothing to do but count the strings on his racket until play could restart.

By the following year Frawley must have decided that the only way to counter such intimidatory tactics was to get involved in the fray, and so establish for all to see that the man on the other side of the net was no sucker. In 1982 McEnroe and Frawley were doubles opponents. McEnroe, still unable or unwilling to keep the lid on his emotions, was having an argument with the umpire when Frawley intervened by walking up to the umpire and saying, calmly but clearly:

'I am going to report you.'

The umpire and McEnroe turned in astonishment. Frawley explained:

'I am going to report you because you didn't put the clock on him.' He gestured at McEnroe.

Frawley was entirely within his rights to invoke the rule that limits interruptions in play to thirty seconds. More important from his point of view, he was sending a clear signal to McEnroe, without having to speak directly to him, that he had rumbled McEnroe's ploy and was prepared to put an official stop to it.

I am convinced that Frawley was taking a sensible line. We hear continually about the problems of the player who stirs everything up by arguing with all and sundry. What we do not hear so much about is the effect this has on his opponent. If anything, this is the more serious issue in that the other player, the innocent party, stands to suffer more than the aggressor. The longer the complaining is allowed to go on, the more the opponent gets left out in the cold. He may suffer physically from this enforced immobility, because it is very easy in those circumstances for a muscle to seize up. He is almost certain to suffer psychologically, because while Mr Loudmouth is keeping up his adrenalin flow through his verbal dispute with the match officials, his opponent's supply of adrenalin is draining away through lack of involvement.

In thinking about this problem, I have come to the conclusion that the innocent player must take steps to protect himself, and that the best way for him to do this is to force himself into the argument. This way his flow of adrenalin is maintained until the dispute is settled.

How should you do this if it happened to you? Rod Frawley's approach was one method, but perhaps he did not need to be quite so indirect. It would be quite permissible to walk up to the umpire and make a direct complaint about an opponent, for example by saying:

'Umpire, I can't concentrate under these conditions. My opponent is complaining and arguing all the time. How can we stop him?'

In those few words you have bought yourself straight into the argument – and without causing any offence. As like as not, the noisy player will start to justify himself, and you can then turn to him and say:

'Look, we're out here to see who is the better tennis player. Why don't you just go back there and play tennis, and we'll see who comes out the winner?'

In a tournament, you would do well to make sure you spoke loudly enough for your challenge to come over on the microphone. Any reasonable crowd will be drawn to support you, since you have implanted in their minds the idea that you are the straight player and that your opponent has to adopt his dubious tactics because he is afraid of losing an honest confrontation. That is why he has been acting up – to throw you off your game.

If this does not work, and he still goes on complaining, you would be quite justified in asking to speak to the referee. You say:

'Umpire, I feel my opponent is deliberately trying to obstruct my concentration and my game. I would like the referee to come out here, please, so we can talk about it.'

You have not been impolite, you have not yelled at anyone. But, instead of sitting back and letting your opponent play tunes on your nerve-ends, you have asserted your right to play a straightforward contest. You have not compromised your ideal that the true name of the game is to win, but you have reminded everyone present that the way a player wins is no less important.

Few tennis crowds overdo it like the Italians. In terms of noise, style, enjoyment, and wildly partisan behaviour they have few equals. When they are the home crowd at a Davis Cup match, they have no equals.

In 1976 I had to play the deciding match in Rome against Adriano Panatta. It was my last appearance in Davis Cup tennis. The crowd were their usual strident near-delirious selves, going overboard with joy every time Panatta, the national hero, won a point – and to their credit granting the Australian visitor a small ripple of applause when he won something.

I took the first set 7–5. In the second set I had my chances but failed to take them. With the score at 6–7, Panatta gained a set point, and won it. It was then my turn, with no change of ends, to serve the first point of the third set. I *would have* served it, that is – but I could not. The crowd would not allow it. They were still barely halfway through all the celebrating they apparently had to do to mark Panatta's victory in the second set.

'Adri-aaano,' sang about twenty thousand voices. 'Adri-aaano.' The noise swelled and faded all round the great bowl of the stadium. Down at the bottom of the bowl I waited helplessly to continue the match.

The chanting of 'Adri-aaano' was succeeded by a sharper, shorter war cry: 'Pa-na-tta! Pa-na-tta! Pa-na-tta!' The crowd whipped themselves into a new frenzy and the idea grew in my mind that I was being ritually burned at the stake by members of a wild pagan tribe. 'Pa-na-tta! Pa-na-tta!' It throbbed round the stadium, a booming savage sound with three distinct movements. I watched their intent, chanting faces, bobbing up and down above heaving shoulders, as though mesmerized. 'Pa-na-tta!' Wave upon wave of them. I thought: 'They *are* crazy. .'

Rescue, when it came, was by the grace of culture. Up behind the umpire's stand was an opera singer, and when he started to let rip most of

the others were silenced by the awful magnitude of the noise that this one man could generate. But even opera singers have to breathe, and in the pauses while he sucked in great balloons of air, the Roman zoo reasserted itself: bawling, yelling, crooning, swooning, throwing cushions and flowers on the court – they would do anything, it seemed, so long as it held up the tennis.

Still unable to resume play, I began to see the humour of the scene. There were all these Italians having the time of their lives just because their man had managed to level the score at 1–1. It was incredible, and I shook my head a few times and laughed at their lunacy. Perhaps I could show them a thing or two yet.

I waited until the umpire at last had brought the crowd under control and they began to be silent. Now their eyes turned to me as I prepared to serve. I gave them a few moments longer, then, as absolute silence took over in the stadium, I threw down my racket and glared up at the crowd.

'Eh!' I shouted, 'what about me?' I gave them an operatic Italian shrug. 'What about-a me, then? Don' I play pretty good?'

They loved it. There was an immediate roar of recognition from the massed ranks of drama-loving Romans. The opera singer was on his feet, competing with a new tribal chant: 'New-combe! New-combe!' It was a full minute before the poor beleaguered umpire at last took charge again and was able to order the third set to begin.

Later in the afternoon I did something – quite unintentionally – that endeared me still more to the Italian crowd. In fact, I became instantly popular throughout the whole of Italy. I lost the match.

he men who figure in this chapter belong to a very special period in Australian tennis history. They have all had brilliant careers as individuals, and as Davis Cup players they helped to create an extraordinary period of Australian dominance through the Fifties and Sixties, when we were hardly ever out of the final round, and in fact came out winners fifteen times between 1950 and 1969. My 'Six' – with the exception of 'Muscles' Rosewall, who seems to have been around for ever – were the mainstays of the national team in the later part of that twenty-year run. What follows is not meant to be a set of formal profiles so much as sketches from memory which, in each case I hope, illuminate certain aspects of the man. Each of the sketches begins with a few memory-jogging career details.

NEALE FRASER Born 1933. Powerful-serving left-hander. Won Wimbledon singles in 1960, US title in 1959, 1960. First played in Davis Cup finals in 1958; captain of first open Davis Cup winners in 1973.

The Davis Cup seems to inspire Australians with a particularly bright fervour. Several times in his career Neale Fraser found himself at the sharp end of Davis Cup competition, either as a player or as team captain, and it is for his efforts for his country that I think he will be remembered most. 'Fraise' wasn't afraid to get deeply involved, and was capable of crying after victory or defeat. In the 1963 Davis Cup finals he came off court a broken man and wept in the dressing-room. There was no denying he had had a bad day in the doubles match against McKinley and Ralston, made to look worse by the storming play of Roy Emerson,

NO. WE'RE NOT EXPECTING RAIN. WE'RE EXPECTING NEALE FRASER

his partner, which almost rescued them; eventually they went down 3–6, 6–4, 9–11, 9–11, and Australia lost the Cup 3–2.

Ten years later, Fraise was captain when we went to Cleveland, Ohio, to try and break a US run of five victories. We beat the Americans 5–0 and at the dinner afterwards, when he accepted the trophy on behalf of the team, he broke down once more. At least, this time, he was able to get his sense of humour back a little more quickly. (I should explain that the unusual spelling of his nickname is deliberate. When we played once in Paris, he showed himself to be a prodigious eater of *fraises*, or strawberries.)

Altogether, 1973 was an eventful Davis Cup year. In one of the earlier rounds we had been drawn against India. We arrived in Madras ten days before the match so we could get acclimatized to the intense heat there. But we soon found that the weather was not to be the greatest of our worries. On the third day, I was resting in my hotel room after practising in the morning, when the phone rang. It was Fraise, asking me to come down to a team meeting. When I arrived, the others were all there, also a stranger, a huge black guy in military uniform, a kind of Sidney Poitier of the Subcontinent. Fraise said:

'We've got a bit of a problem. The colonel here will tell you about it.'

The black guy began to explain that his office had received word from Interpol that a death threat was to be made against the Australian team. The group responsible were campaigning for the release of Pakistani soldiers taken prisoner in the recent war. To promote their cause they had decided to create an international incident, and apparently they had hit on the idea of wiping out the visiting Australian tennis team.

The colonel explained all this, adding that it was up to us to decide whether or not we should leave the country and maybe try and stage the match somewhere else. 'But,' he said finally, drawing himself up to his full height, 'if you stay, and a bullet comes, it comes through here first.' He stabbed with a finger at his great barrel chest. 'And if a knife comes, it also comes through here first.'

He was trying to relax us, of course. When he'd gone, it fell to Fraise to chair the meeting at which we decided whether to leave or stay. We decided to stay, told our Indian hosts and then stood back while they mounted a vast security campaign. They cleared everyone else off our floor in the hotel, and stationed armed guards next to the lift. At the main entrance to the hotel they put a machine-gunner, and all the other entrances were guarded with armed men. Everywhere else you could think of, they had plain-clothes security men falling over each other. Whenever we went to the courts we travelled in a police car with another in front and one behind. There were security men all round the practice courts, and at the stadium – a 10,000-seater made of bamboo which they had erected specially in two weeks – our hosts had a main force of 300 armed men.

All the same, I couldn't help thinking in the occasional lonely moment that it would take only one determined man with a gun to upset all these heart-warming security arrangements. In the stadium there was no wind and the outdoor temperature was really fierce, about 130 degrees; as we played, the blood in our bodies must have been near boiling point. If we'd been hit by a bullet, we'd have bled to death in seconds.

Thankfully, no-one tried it. We got through the match, and afterwards flew, still accompanied by armed guards, from Madras to Calcutta. We stayed the night in Calcutta, and next day drove out to the airport to catch our plane home. On the steps of the aircraft we said goodbye to our last contingent of security men. It would be difficult to say who looked more relieved, them or us. Phew! Goodbye India. (As it happens, I haven't been back there since.)

Later, as we reminisced about our ten-day prison sentence in the Madras hotel – which we'd never left except to go and play tennis – we thought again of Colonel Bullet-Comes-Through-Here-First. And wondered why we'd never seen him again since that first day . . .

So, thank you, Neale Fraser. We had a few good trips together, didn't we?

ROY EMERSON Born 1936. Athletic right-hander. Won Wimbledon singles in 1964, 1965, US title in 1961, 1964, French title in 1963, 1965, Australian title in 1961, 1963–67. Noted doubles player. Appeared in 18 Davis Cup ties.

'Emmo' was our fitness king in the Davis Cup team. Where the rest of us might practise for four hours, then run two miles and do some stomach work (sit-ups and so forth), Emmo would practise with the team, come off court and run five miles, then do more stomach work than the rest of us put together.

I was caught up in the Emerson way of training when we went to play a Davis Cup match in Sweden. The year before, I had met a girl in Hamburg (I was to marry her two years later). Because Hamburg and Sweden are so close, I decided to ask Harry Hopman, our coach, if she could come over to watch the match. 'Hop', ever the strict disciplinarian, wasn't going to make it easy for me. We were out having dinner with the rest of the team, and Hop decided to take a team vote on it.

'Who's in favour?' he asked.

Roche and Davidson put up their hands. Two votes for me (I wasn't allowed to vote, though).

'Against?'

Stolle and Emerson put up their hands. That made it two votes for each side, leaving Hopman, by the way he'd rigged it, with the casting vote. Hop sucked his teeth for a bit, and put on a sorrowful expression.

'Well,' he said finally, 'I guess that means she can't come.' He looked at me. 'I dunno,' he said, pausing. 'There may just be one way she can come. If you're willing to do everything that Roy does in training . . .'

Even though the whole thing was a set-up, I had no bargaining position and had to agree to match Emerson in training every day for the next week.

On the first morning, we had to run three or four miles down through the farm properties beside the beach, then back again. Emerson was soon in the lead, and each time we came to a farmer's gate, he'd hurdle it. A few yards behind, I was reaching the gate, pushing it open, closing it behind me, starting up again. The gap between us widened with every gate we came to. At the far end of the run, he stripped off, sprinted into the sea and swam out a couple of hundred yards and back, while I lay spread on the sand like an asphyxiated starfish, trying to recover. Then we ran back. All in all, it was a week to remember!

My other problem with Emmo (apart from the fact that he is seven years older than me) was on the tennis court, where for years I couldn't

WHEN SHE GETS HERE — I'LL STRANGLE HER!

THAT WAS A NICE SMILE YOU GOT FROM THE ROYAL BOX

beat him. The first thirteen times we played each other, he won. Then, at last, in 1967 I beat him. We met again in 1970 in a memorable quarter-final at Wimbledon. Memorable not only because it was a tough five-setter, but also for an incident at the start of the fourth set. He was leading two sets to one, and we were playing a long deuce game on my service, with advantages being won and lost on both sides. Then, athletic as ever, Emmo chased a wide ball and finished up in the stand with the spectators. Not only that, he broke the fastening on his pants in the process. Fortunately, the Wimbledon crowd are a reasonably kind bunch of people, and he was able to persuade someone to lend him a safety pin so he could do some temporary repairs and continue the match. Even after that he didn't slow up, and the match went on into the fifth set, when I finally beat him 11–9 after four hours and forty minutes' play. That's not bad, when you think about it, for a man who for almost two sets never knew from one moment to the next whether his pants weren't going to plummet to the grass.

Emmo, however, was not the man to be fazed by that kind of experience. He was a great practical joker in the dressing-room, and he and I sometimes joined forces. In 1970 a professional charity tournament, rather grandly called the World Cup, was launched between teams from the United States and Australia. In the beginning it was a kind of substitute Davis Cup for the pros. The players took it very seriously, and there was big rivalry between the two teams. From 1972 the matches were played at Hartford, Connecticut, and every time Emmo and I got there we'd chalk up his old school war cry on a blackboard in the dressing-room – knowing that the Americans were in the adjoining room. After a winning match, we went back to the dressing-room, got right up close to the door leading to the Americans, and screamed out the war cry. This is how it went:

> Wong wong, tara ya,
> Light dark, ya ya.
> Rang rang, murray gum,
> Coom coom, carry gum,
> Moll moll tipparoo,
> Honalu, honalu,
> We're the boys of the kangaroo!

The Americans, I need hardly tell you, used to love it, and would reply with strangled cries of 'Wait till next year, you bastards!' and other, less cultured material. Still, Emmo and I quite enjoyed it.

ROD LAVER Born 1938. Attacking left-hander. Only player to achieve amateur and open Grand Slams, in 1962, 1969. Won Wimbledon singles in 1961, 1962, 1968, 1969, US title in 1962, 1969, French title in 1962, 1969, Australian title in 1960, 1962, 1969. Played in five Davis Cup-winning sides.

Rod the Rocket, so nicknamed by coach Harry Hopman when he was anything but that, matured into one of the most successful players of all time. Off-court he is a likeable, straightforward guy, and over the years we have had our share of beers together. But it is Rod the player I would like to give an account of here. For me, he is the one player I could never fancy my chances against, particularly when we came to the final stages in a five-setter. Five-set matches were my *forte*, but when Laver and I got into the fifth set he had this very rare ability to change gear suddenly, produce something extra and carry the day. We might get to 4–4, or 5–5, then he'd pull off a stroke that turned the match. I had my wins against him, in fact I was the last amateur to beat him before he turned professional in 1962. But if there is one contest that for me best illustrates the artistry of Rod Laver, it is a challenge match we played one night in Rochester, New York.

I was down two sets to love, won the next two sets and we reached 3-all in the fifth set. All night I had been coming in and hitting the first volley down to his backhand and he had countered this by trying to pass me or play lobs over my backhand side. That had been his game all night. We stood at 30-all in the seventh game. I came in and hit the ball to his backhand and moved in to the net. He drew back his racket to play the lob shot, and as I saw this I began to shift my weight backwards to my left, expecting to have to run back for the lob. He went into the ball shaping to play it in exactly the same way as he had been doing all night – until he got to the ball. Then he turned the lob into a chip shot.

It wasn't designed to go for a winner; what he was aiming for was to set himself up for the next shot. Now, as the ball came towards me, I couldn't play the shot I'd planned. My weight was still inclined backwards, so I couldn't get it fully behind the volley; I'd have to play it just with the arm. The next problem I had to decide in about a millisecond was: *where* do I hit it? Laver was at the back of the court. If I hit it back down the line to him, he could play his whipped topspin

backhand across the court, and I wouldn't be able to get over in time to cover it. If I played the ball across to his forehand I couldn't hit it hard enough; my weight wouldn't be in the shot and he'd be able to hit a forehand winner. There was a third option. If I hit it down the middle, and got it deep, I'd be able to recover, get back to the centre of the court and be in a good position to reply. I went for the deep shot down the middle . . . and hit it out by about three inches.

When the volley went out, I applauded his previous shot. He had done it again. Suckered me in for three hours to expect a certain kind of play, then changed up to another gear and beat me. That was the magic of Rod Laver.

 FRED STOLLE Born 1938. Competitive right-hander. Three times singles runner-up at Wimbledon, in 1963–65. Won US singles title in 1966, French title in 1965. Outstanding doubles player. Won 13 Davis Cup rubbers out of 16.

Fred must be one of my greatest fans. Although he has never admitted this publicly, I feel it's time he received proper acknowledgment for the exceptional amount of time he has spent thinking up new ways to praise me. To give you just a brief example of his style, he has long admired my range of backhand shots, and in 1968 we were face to face in the Wimbledon doubles final. My partner was Roche, his was Rosewall.

First point of the match: Rosewall to serve with Stolle up at the net. Rosewall hit one down the middle, I swung my racket and just slammed into the ball as hard as I could. The ball flew past Stolle down the line – probably the hardest backhand winner I've ever hit in my life.

While the crowd applauded, and Roche dropped his racket and began to laugh, I took the opportunity to point out to Fred that it was a waste of time serving balls like that, to my strong side. Fred, too, had dropped his racket. 'Right,' he declared. 'We won't have to worry about that shot any more – now that you've hit your one for the year!'

Nowadays, you seldom hear that kind of spontaneous generosity. But Fred hasn't given up, and I do my best to return his compliments.

More recently, we played the US doubles together in 1981 and got through to the semi-finals, losing to McEnroe and Fleming on a tie-break in the fifth set. The tournament was being covered on television by CBS, and I was also working for them at the time. The progress of the veterans Stolle and Newcombe had been attracting large crowds, and after Fred and I had won our quarter-final, we came off court and someone from CBS ran over and asked me to interview Fred. I was delighted to oblige, so I took the microphone and said to him:

'Well, Fred, congratulations on your fine win today. There must have been a lot of middle-aged men like yourself sitting out there watching the match. I'm sure they would really enjoy hearing your secret for everlasting life. I mean, how does a bloke as old as you manage to play so well?'

'Oh,' said Fred. 'It's nothing special. I have a few beers each night and just . . . hang in there loose, you know.'

SHAME AGAIN BARMAN — I'M ON THE SHTOLLE WIMBLEDON TRAINING COURSH . . . . .

This, and more, went out live to the viewers, and we carried on through the week in that kind of relaxed vein. A few weeks after the tournament, I was down in Florida and did an interview for a local paper. Their reporter asked me about my plans for the following year, and whether I'd be back for the doubles. I said:

'Yes, I'd like to come back next year, but I'm not sure if I'll be playing with Stolle. I've been a little upset lately with his training habits. He goes out partying every night and is always drinking too much beer. I mean, if I played with him again I'd probably have to go on a weightlifting course before the tournament, I get so exhausted having to carry him for two weeks. You see my problem, don't you?'

It wasn't until some four months later that I actually saw this interview in print, after a friend had sent me a cutting. I thought Fred would be interested to see it, too, so I underlined what seemed to be the main points of the article, in red ink, and sent off the cutting to him. That was in about March 1982. I didn't get a reply, but a little while later Fred, who lives in Florida, was doing a broadcast on the French championships. It was my birthday during the week of the final rounds, and during a break in play Fred suddenly seemed to remember something.

'Oh, yes,' he said to the listeners. 'A lot of great Australians have won the French title. One who didn't win it was, of course, John Newcombe. And talking about him reminds me, it was his birthday yesterday. So I'd just like to wish him many happy returns on his 43rd birthday.'

In fact it was my 38th birthday. The gesture, though, was typical of the man: he'd sat there quietly for several weeks, planning his revenge. To date, I haven't seen him since that broadcast went out. When I do, I may have a reply ready . . .

Not surprisingly, I have known about Fred and his ways for a long time. Way back, almost at the beginning of my doubles partnership with Tony Roche, we received a lesson in pre-match conditioning that probably served us well in the years to come. On that occasion, Fred's partner was Roy Emerson.

It was 1965, and we had reached the final of the French doubles. Tony and I had an early night and arrived at the courts two hours before the match. We practised, had a workout and felt as well prepared as we'd ever been. I was then twenty, Tony was nineteen, and it was a very big occasion for us.

Eventually Stolle and Emerson – both several years older than us – arrived in the dressing-room. They went round the corner from us to change, but their voices were loud enough for us to overhear what they were saying. The main topic was their hangovers. As the groaning and cursing floated round the corner to Tony and myself, we exchanged looks of triumph. If they'd been out that late, and felt as bad as they said, we had it made.

Half an hour later, after we'd taken the first set, we really felt we

.... AND BEST ACTOR AWARDS — STOLLE AND EMERSON ....

were on our way to our first Big Four doubles title. The other guys had blown up already. Tony and I grinned confidently at each other.

Three sets later, the match was over – and *we* were the also-rans. Stolle and Emerson were looking remarkably fit for a pair of self-confessed crocks as they accepted the trophy. Later, as Tony and I reviewed the match, we reached the unanimous verdict that if our opponents had gone out the night before, they must have come in again half an hour later, that if they'd had hangovers they must have earned them from drinking, at most, two glasses of watery French beer, that, in short, we'd been superbly conned. Our only consolation was that now, at least, we knew how it was done – and could start doing it to others!

KEN ROSEWALL Born 1934. Evergreen right-handed natural left-hander. Though dominant in three decades of championship tennis, he never won the Wimbledon singles but was runner-up four times, in 1954, 1956, 1970, 1974. Won US singles title in 1956, 1970, French title in 1953, 1968, Australian title in 1953, 1955, 1971, 1972. Played in four Davis Cup-winning teams between 1953 and 1973.

If Kenny Rosewall was ever perturbed at being tagged 'Muscles' in the course of his extraordinary career, he has never let it show. Perhaps he felt, as his youthful, bony, upward-tapering body began to fill out, that the sardonic nickname had become redundant. In any event, it was not in his nature to be easily deflected from the main business in

hand, which with him was to win tennis matches. Let the others do the fooling, he was content to plug away on the circuit, amassing trophies, honours, and much else besides. Somewhere inside that small frame there has always been an ultra-competitive spirit that, even with the approach of his half-a-hundredth birthday, refuses to be extinguished.

I have first-hand, up-to-the-minute experience of the Rosewall brand of never-say-die. He lives just a couple of miles from me in Sydney, and he comes round to practise with me on my court. At least, I like to think of it as practice; but Kenny insists on treating practice as if it was a five-set final on the Centre Court at Wimbledon or down in the bull-pit at Flushing Meadow. The upshot is: I always lose. I wouldn't mind that so much, except that it is *my* court we always play on. Kenny hasn't got a court of his own. He tells me from time to time that he's trying to buy a plot of land for a court from the lady next door, but she's holding out on him.

I can sympathize with that. At least, I did until the day he started to point out that holes were appearing in my net, and hadn't I better get them fixed? As I watched him poking the handle of his racket through some of the larger gaps in my net, and glancing up at me with something very like reproach in his eyes, it just struck me that, yes, there *were* holes in my net, but if he objected to them more strongly than I did, could he not possibly just buy us a new net? At least then he wouldn't have to complain about the old one.

I needn't have worried. Kenny must have read my thoughts because, a few days later, he turned up at the court with his own special answer to the problem. Not a new net exactly, but something very much in that direction. From his bag he took a great pile of shoelaces – old shoelaces – and set about repairing the holes in my net with them. I was quite touched: he must have immobilized at least twenty pairs of old tennis shoes to assemble a repair outfit on that scale. Ah well, I thought to myself, that's friendship for you.

The net's fine now. It looks a bit different from most tennis nets, what with the loose ends of shoelace hanging off it, but I like it. Nowadays if there's a cloud at all in the atmosphere when we play, it's just that Muscles is still so competitive about our games and insists on winning. Of course, I don't want him to think I'm ungrateful to him for patching up the net. I am *extremely* grateful. All the same, it is *my* court, and if he doesn't let me win one day soon I may have to ask him not to come around anymore.

TONY ROCHE Born 1945. Combative left-hander. Runner-up in Wimbledon singles in 1968, runner-up in US singles in 1969, 1970, won French title in 1966. Outstanding record as doubles player, with John Newcombe, including five Wimbledon titles, one US, three French and four Australian. Regular Davis Cup player from 1965.

In 1965 I got engaged in Hamburg to the girl I later married. There was a party to celebrate, to which the Australian boys were all invited, and next morning I wasn't feeling very well at all. But, hangover or not, I was down to play doubles with Tony. I went out on court shading my eyes, and tried to warm up. As Tony prepared to serve, I had the feeling it was going to be a difficult day. I was squinting fiercely over the net, when, with his opening serve, Tony hit me full-square on the back of the head. It's the only time he's ever done it in all the years we've played together. The ball pinged about a hundred feet up in the air, and my head throbbed violently for the rest of the day.

It was simply one of those moments of bad luck – or so I have always assumed. If you play doubles with someone for any length of time, it doesn't improve the relationship if you swear at them every time something goes wrong. Nevertheless Tony *did* have quite a lot of defensive work to do in our early years, particularly while I was going through a phase in my life when I kept buying things from joke-shops.

One summer we were travelling in the United States. We were on a plane and Tony knew that I had one of those balloon cushions which

make a noise like a fart when you sit on them. His problem was, he didn't know where the cushion was so he could grab it off me, nor did he know when or how I was going to use it on him. After a while he said:

'I'm going to the toilet.'

'Great,' I said. 'I'm really happy for you.'

'No,' he said, 'I'm telling you that because I know you're going to do something to my seat while I'm away. So don't bother trying to do it.'

I said: 'I don't know what you're talking about.'

Before he went, I noticed that he was careful to arrange his seat in such a way that he'd be able to tell if it had been disturbed when he came back. While he was away, I rearranged things a little, but without putting anything under the seat.

When Tony came back, he looked down to check his seat and said to me sternly:

'All right, come on. Take it out.'

I said: 'What are you talking about? There's nothing in there.'

Tony didn't want to suffer the indignity of rooting around in his seat like a madman, and maybe set the thing off in the process, so he stood in the aisle and tried to stare me into removing it myself. I did nothing. Then the stewardess came down the aisle pushing her trolley, but had to stop because Tony was blocking the way. She asked him if he'd mind moving over and Tony said no, he couldn't do that. She asked why and Tony replied:

'I can't move in there and sit down because this guy (pointing at me) has put something under my seat.'

I turned an innocent face to the stewardess and said: 'I'm sorry, I don't even know this person. And I certainly haven't touched his seat.'

'Sure,' said Tony, with a faint snarl. He'd had enough of this play-acting. He reached down and gave the seat a violent jerk, exposing the underside. 'There!' he began to say, then took another look. His jaw fell. I started to laugh.

Eventually we landed at Shreveport, Louisiana, where we were to play an exhibition match the next day. The tennis officials met us at the airport and took us to our accommodation. It was in a private house and

the owner, a lady, welcomed us and showed us to our bedroom. There were two single beds in the room, and a bathroom adjoining. It was getting late and so we prepared to go to bed.

Tony had somehow known about the existence of the farting cushion. What he didn't know was that I was also carrying one of those plastic shapes, mainly grey-brown in colour, which when placed on the floor look exactly like vomit.

I waited until Tony had gone to sleep, then I put this thing down on the carpet near the foot of his bed where he couldn't miss it. I went to sleep.

I awoke several hours later to cries of 'Oh, no! That's disgusting! Oh, my God, no!' Tony had got up to go to the bathroom, come back and found my lump of plastic lying in wait for him. The sight of vomit is something Tony particularly loathes, so there was no question of him being practical and trying to clear it up. While he was still reeling about from the shock, I asked him what was the matter.

'Eugh! Somebody's been sick on the floor here.'

I said: 'You've got to be kidding!' I jumped out of bed and went over to look. 'Oh, no!' I cried, 'that's really disgusting.' I stood there for a while making sympathetic noises, then I hopped back into bed.

After a while I suggested to Tony that maybe it was a dog or some animal who'd done it. On the other hand, the bedroom door was shut. How could a dog have got in and done it while we were sleeping? Tony nodded morosely. The whole thing was getting much too complicated for that hour of the night – or was it morning?

'Hey,' I said, struck by a new thought, 'maybe it *was* a dog. And the dog's still *here* in the room!'

Tony agreed at once. His first instinct was to jump back inside the comforting protection of his bed. Then a few seconds later (it was almost too good to be true) he decided to settle the mystery. He pushed back the covers and leaned down towards the floor. He started peering around for some sign of the dog, a tail maybe, sticking out from under the wardrobe. He began whistling softly and calling:

'Here, boy, here. Here, boy.'

By this time I was cracking up inside, but I just managed to keep the laughter down long enough to suggest to Tony that he should go out and find the woman who owned the house. Get her to come and clean it up. Tell her it wasn't us, it must have been a dog or something.

Tony considered this for a while. Should he go out and risk the wrath of our landlady? It was still barely daylight. Would she believe it had been a dog if no dog could be found? Suppose she didn't have a dog? She'd probably deny having one anyway, be too embarrassed to admit she'd allowed it to happen.

The scene lasted about fifteen minutes. It ended when suddenly I couldn't hold back the laughter any more. As I exploded, Tony swung round on me. His heart sank at what he saw: his doubles partner hissing and trembling like a burst boiler – and for the *second* time in twenty-four hours. Was he stuck with this man forever? What else did he have in his luggage?

(For further adventures with Rochey, see also 'The Russian Incident,' 'Agents and Company' and 'Oriental Magic.')

We looked the property over with sinking hearts. Could this delapidated dude ranch ever be cleaned up and converted into a place where people would really want to come and stay with their families for a week or two of concentrated tennis? If you have ever gone to view a run-down property, you will know the feeling. It *is* difficult to go and view a place for the first time – even if you have seen photographs of it – and not carry along in your head some wonderful mental picture of the renovated version you plan to build. You turn a bend in the road – and there stands the real thing. Ugly, clapped-out, neglected; no-one's home.

With us there was the added problem of scale. The main lodge had sixteen rooms. Outside, a bunch of horses (cast-offs from the dude ranch) roamed loose in two hundred acres. How on earth could we knock all that land into shape? Where would we begin? A lot more deliberation followed, which eventually got us to the stage of agreeing that we *would* begin. Somehow.

With me in the venture were my wife and two business associates, Jack Turpin and tennis coach Clarence Maybury. It was 1968, I had just turned professional, and was looking for two different things which I hoped to be able to combine in the tennis ranch.

First was the need to create a second home, probably in the US where I would be playing most of my tennis from now on. In winter we could go back to Sydney, Australia, but in the main playing season it would be essential to have a real base closer to the heart of the pro tennis circuit. We rejected the idea of joining the high-lifers on the East or West Coast, and (until we saw the place) felt much more attracted to the idea of living somewhere like where the ranch was – near a quiet town in Texas, about thirty miles from San Antonio.

The second thing I was looking for was a way out of the tunnel-vision life of the tennis circuit. To help develop a business would

get me out of that repetitive sequence of hotel-practice-play-hotel-party-travel-another hotel, etc. I knew, from watching the effect on some of the older players, that meeting the bigger world outside that cosy, inward-looking circuit could be, when the time came and if you weren't prepared for it, an uncomfortable shock. A tennis ranch, moreover, offered the chance to learn about business while still operating in the familiar surroundings of tennis coaching.

We set to work. We washed it down, cleaned it out, extended it, painted it, installed tennis courts and guest accommodation in the grounds, and one day several months later we were open for business. In the first six years I spent a lot of time down at the ranch – to the point where some of the players on the circuit told me I was crazy, going off to a ranch in Texas when there was such good money to be earned playing pro tennis day in and day out, nights as well. I just felt they were proving my argument *for* going down to the ranch.

Good evening, ladies

Since those first pioneering, horseshit-shovelling days, the ranch has grown into a solid establishment with thirty courts and accommodation for two hundred visitors. (It is also the home of the world's largest moustache, described earlier.) Mainly the people who come are family groups; they spend most of the day out on the tennis courts, then in the evenings they have dinner in the lodge and maybe a few drinks afterwards. On Saturdays we usually have a band, so people can dance if they have any energy left.

Actually, energy is one thing our visitors to the ranch are rarely short of. In the early days, as I well remember, we held a lot of four-day ladies' clinics, from which I used to need three days to recover.

They came in from the cities, from Dallas and Houston. Well-to-do society ladies, aged from thirty to fifty-five, fresh from the swimming pools, gymnasia, spiritual massage and body-toning parlors that are essential to life in Texas today – and, boy, they gave me a hard time.

Out on the courts they ran and played like demons. But it was in the evenings that they really let their hair down. We did not have a great many amusement facilities at the lodge, so after dinner we had to improvise. A couple of drinks prepared the way – and then it was party time!

One of the favourite games we played in the hall of the lodge was an obstacle relay race. At the start of the race, the ladies lined up in two teams. On the word 'Go', they had to run to the first table and swallow a drink. Then they had to crawl under the table, run to the end of the hall (by the men's toilet), get down on their hands and knees, crawl under the door and touch the men's toilet, crawl out, get up, run around a big wooden table until they came to a line of three long tables. They had to dive up on these tables and do an army crawl to the other end, then jump off, run back to the start-line and tag their team-mate who was next in the line. Then off she went.

It sounds corny, maybe, but it had an irresistible appeal for the ladies. I was constantly staggered to see how these socialites jumped the tables, crawled round the floor, bumped, pulled, tripped and in many other ingenious ways foully impeded their opponents. It was like a wild saloon scene from some Western, staged in the Ol' Texas. A privilege to watch.

I n the early 1970s the world tennis map consisted of Europe, America and Australia. There were a few outposts elsewhere, but no tournaments of international stature. The professional season was similarly patchy; the French, Wimbledon and US championships were the highlights of the circuit in the summer months, then there was a big gap until Christmas, when the Australian championships were held.

In November 1972 Fred Stolle and I were flying back to Australia from London. We were talking, not for the first time, about the problems of having to play most of our tennis on the other side of the world from where our homes were. Why couldn't there be some tournaments closer to home, played in October–November? The level of interest in professional tennis had taken off in the previous five years, but there was still no circuit at all in the Far East. We started to speculate on what we might do.

From home I wrote to a number of people I knew in the East. At the beginning of 1973 I went on a tour there and was able to get people to agree to organize tournaments on a circuit that included Japan, Hong Kong, the Philippines and Indonesia. These countries had a few small tournaments already, but each was very much an individual event. The organizers had the will, but lacked the know-how to set up something on a larger scale. That was where I was able to help, advising them on what could be done and how to go about doing it.

Despite a move to block the new circuit, I secured the necessary permission from the International Lawn Tennis Federation and by May 1973 we were in business. At least, *they* were in business. Although a lot of people seemed to assume that I stood to make a lot of money out of the Far Eastern venture, in fact I had failed to ask anyone out there for a cent for helping to organize it. The only tournament that involved me financially was an associated one, the Australian Indoor Championships, which I set up with Fred Stolle. And there Fred and I wondered for a time

if we hadn't stuck our heads in a noose, because until we found a sponsor (which was not until two months before the event!) we had to guarantee the $50,000 prize money ourselves. For a while we felt we could be scheduled for the high jump, but a sponsor did eventually come along and the Indoor event, along with the Far Eastern circuit, is now established as a regular part of the tennis calendar.

Crowds were enthusiastic and gratifyingly large from the beginning. When I played Rosewall in the final in Japan the stadium was packed with 11,000 people. For the players, it was a whole new experience. To me personally, the wonder of going to the Far East each year was how different the various centres were from each other. To travel from the Philippines to Taiwan was to enter a completely fresh world, with different customs, a different mentality, different food, a different lifestyle altogether. If you went from there to Japan, you met another completely different set of circumstances. Each year brought new revelations – and entertainments.

Night games

One of the highlights in Hong Kong was a rickshaw race. We held it at about four o'clock in the morning in Nathan Road, which runs through the middle of the city. We put the rickshaw boys in the seats behind and pulled the rickshaws ourselves. The boys in the back thought it was pretty funny being ringside spectators at a half-mile drag race through the city in the hour before dawn. We thought it was pretty exhausting.

In Djakarta they have rickshaws too. I travelled by rickshaw the night I met the most embarrassed man I have ever seen. Our all-male, all-Australian party of ten climbed aboard a small fleet of the flimsy vehicles and someone gave the command: 'Take us to the Houses of Ill Repute.'

The rickshaw boys led us down to a dark canal. Beside the canal stood a row of scruffy-looking huts. We dismounted and charged into the largest of the huts, there to find a timid-looking Englishman in the process of bargaining with the Madame. Around the two of them stood the girls, and he had evidently reached that stage of the ritual where he had to select his girl. At such delicate moments, I guess, the last thing a

timid Englishman wishes to meet is a herd of shouting yelling
Australians. He could not have looked guiltier if we'd found him on the
floor without his trousers. We didn't stay long, just stamped about for five
minutes or so and took off, back to the rickshaws. But behind us we left a
shattered man. Our visit must have destroyed his night. In fact, *we*

probably finished up more exhausted than he did. We had another rickshaw race.

I'm thinking of taking it up professionally. We could start a circuit for tourists; there's probably a huge untapped market out there. We could go in with a hotel group, set up an itinerary, rent a few dozen rickshaws and run it like a travelling tennis ranch. We'd have to take a few rickshaw-pulling lessons first, though . . . 'Operator, I want to call a Mr Fred Stolle . . .'

PLENTY MORE ROOM ON TOP!

The faith healers

The inside of my right elbow was hurting badly. It had been giving me pain for two months, but as I came off court in Manila after losing my semi-final there in 1974, it hurt just to throw my racket on the dressing-room floor. I decided: 'Right, that's it. I'm going to the faith healer'.

At 7.30 next morning I was in his operating room. For moral support I had three guys with me, also the knowledge that Tony Roche had been successfully operated on for an elbow complaint the previous year – though, admittedly, he had gone to a different faith healer. We would see.

The healer was called Juan Blanché. He examined my elbow; in the crook there was a puffy bluish area about the size of a dollar coin. Blanché indicated that he would operate at that spot. To make his incision, he took hold of the index finger of one of my companions and positioned it about eight inches away from my elbow, and pointing at it. He gazed for several seconds at the finger and the injured arm, then grasped the finger by the middle joint and moved it sharply through the air. Eight inches away, a small incision about an inch and half long appeared on the inside of my elbow. There had been no physical contact whatsoever between the finger and my arm.

Blanché used the opening to extract some gooey, spongy material from the flesh, and in a short while the operation

WHEN DID YOU LAST CUT YOUR NAILS ?

56

was complete. The bluish colour on that part of the elbow was gone. In time the skin healed over, and I was cured. All that now remains is a faint scar.

When I compared my experience with Tony's, I found that the faith healers of the Philippines do not conform to identical methods. His man, called Placido, worked in Baguio some three hundred miles north of Manila. He performed an operation similar to the one I had – also on an injured elbow – but when he had finished working he closed up Tony's wound, and from that moment there was no visible sign that an incision had been made. Before going to see Placido, Tony had twice submitted to the knives of orthodox Western surgeons without success. Since going to Placido, Tony has never had an arm problem.

If you think I understand it, you couldn't be more wrong. I have read several books about faith healers, but their evidence is not conclusive. I also went back there with an American surgeon, and we spent some weeks observing faith healers at work – though again we could form no conclusions. Back home, people heard about my experience and started telling me theirs. A lot claimed they had been helped by similar treatments, but a lot had been disappointed. Others sought my advice. Should they go to the Philippines to try and cure their arthritis, housemaid's knee, lumbago, warts, allergies? I could only say: 'Look. I know what happened to me. But it doesn't always work. If you want to take the risk, that must be your choice.'

Three years after my operation, I was again in the Philippines and was invited with three other tennis players – Martina Navratilova, Evonne Cawley and Ilie Nastase – to meet President Marcos. We were with him in his office for about forty-five minutes, and he spent thirty of them talking to me about the faith healers. He said they had received such huge publicity that he had asked for one of them to be brought to the palace so he could watch an operation. I guess the faith healer would have been pretty nervous that day! Has anyone seen him since?

The telephone rang in my hotel room. It was Tony Roche.

'How are you feeling?' he asked.

'Good,' I said.

'You want to be a millionaire?' he asked.

'Sure,' I replied, 'why not? What's the story?'

'Well,' he explained, 'there's a guy here wants to make us millionaires – if we turn professional.'

'That sounds like a good idea.' I said. 'Where can we meet him in the next two minutes?'

The year was 1967, and we were in New York, halfway through the Forest Hills tournament. Tony and I were then the leading young players on the amateur circuit (later that week I was to take the singles title and Tony and I won the doubles).

The guy making these golden overtures was staying in the same hotel – the Roosevelt – and soon Tony and I were trying not to run down the corridor leading to his suite. Part of the reason for our highly positive reaction to this total stranger's proposal was . . . money. At the time I was receiving $500 from the US Tennis Association for appearing in the championships, and that fee was to cover my air fares, hotel, meals, everything. My wife was with me on the tour as well, so cash wasn't exactly rolling out of our pockets.

The guy we met was a New Orleans promoter named Dave Dixon, and he had an associate with him called Bob Briner. Dave explained that he was in partnership with a very wealthy man, whose name he was not at liberty to reveal, and that they wanted Tony, myself and six other amateurs to turn professional. They wanted us initially for three years. Each year we'd play twenty weeks of tournament tennis and be available to them throughout the year. If we signed with them, they guaranteed us each $45,000 a year for three years.

Hooked

That was the package, beginning in 1968. Tony and I asked for time to

think over the offer, and spent the rest of the day seeing noughts before the eyes and being generally impressed by the view. The next day I had a call from Dave Dixon, who said, in the expansive way of big-time US promoters:

'I want you and Tony to go across the street to Abercrombie and Fitch. Go up to the sixth floor there and ask for Mr Brown. Then you two boys pick out a suit that you like.'

Tony and I thought this was terrific. I was 23 and he was 22, and this Southern gentleman wanted to buy us each a suit. Across we went and picked out our suits. (Mine turned out to be the kind of terrible choice you make when you are in a hurry, or delude yourself into thinking that money is no object; after a couple of outings I hardly wore the thing.)

However, as we strutted about in Abercrombie and Fitch, we were undoubtedly enjoying ourselves. Only later did it dawn on us that we were getting hooked. The suits may have been free, but by accepting them we'd placed ourselves under a moral obligation to the promoter.

About two days later we saw Dave Dixon again, and discussed the deal further. Despite our gullibility over the suits, we did dimly recognize that the decision we were being asked to take was the most important of our entire lives, and we found it very hard to make up our minds. The talks went back and forth with no positive result. Then Dixon disappeared into another room. Twenty minutes later he came back and said that he had spoken to his partner and could tell us that he was Lamar Hunt.

Lamar Hunt was a very wealthy Texas oilman, and it so happened that Tony and I were good friends with Hunt's nephew, Al Hill Jr. Al was also a partner in this tennis deal, which was with a company calling itself World Championship Tennis Inc. We got on the phone and talked to Al Hill Jr, and that made us feel a lot more comfortable about what we were being asked to do. It was an exciting time for us, we were complete novices at the business side of tennis, we were on the verge of agreeing to turn professional . . . all of which may help to explain why what we did next was one of the dumbest acts we've ever committed.

We signed a $1000 option which gave WCT Inc first claim on us as professionals. We weren't turning professional there and then, but should we decide to do so in the future, and there were rival professional groups around, the option meant that WCT had us well and truly stitched up – and all for $1000 apiece. We didn't have to do it, and in fact they needed us more than we needed them. Worse still, as we found out later, they then used our signatures on the option papers to go round to the other top amateurs they wanted to sign – Roger Taylor, Nikki Pilic, Cliff Drysdale and others – and said: 'Look. Here's a virtual agreement from Newcombe and Roche that they're coming in with us.' And that encouraged the other guys to sign up.

Tony and I went back to Australia, and there we decided we'd better take some professional advice. So far we'd been so naive we'd gone in and discussed terms and signed the option papers without consulting anyone: we had neither agent nor lawyer. In Sydney we went to a lawyer friend of mine and it was embarrassing to answer him as he tried to find out how far we'd gone.

'Did you sign anything?' he asked.

'Well . . . not really.'

'Let's put it another way, did you sign *something*?'

'Yeah, there was something. But, you know, it was only an option . . .'

(*Lawyer starts to bang head on desk.*)

Eventually we signed the contract with World Championship Tennis. It turned out OK for us in the end, and we weren't hurt by it. But, in similar circumstances, it could have gone very wrong, and I use that story now to warn the young players I'm involved with what to expect, and to tell them what the proper procedures are so they don't land themselves in dire trouble. The simple truth is, a young player is putty in the hands of a promoter – unless he or she is ready for the attack when it comes, and knows what to say and do. I don't necessarily blame WCT, or outfits like them. In our case, Tony and I were stupid because we didn't try to learn the rules of their game before we started to deal with them.

Managing the managers

For the time being I left my business affairs in the hands of my lawyer friend in Sydney. I had a couple of approaches from IMG – the Mark McCormack Organization – who were then big in golf but hadn't gone into tennis although they were looking at the possibilities. For three years or so I didn't pursue the idea of joining up with an agent, then I did sign a contract with McCormack's International Management Group – and here I learned a few more things about how to cope with managers.

The essential point with sports agents, as with agents in any field, is that you have to be sure that whoever is representing your account is doing the right job for you, understands what you want and can work efficiently with you. Just signing with Mark McCormack's company, for instance, doesn't bring you the undivided attention of Mark McCormack; you are passed on to someone else who is responsible for the day-to-day running of your account. In my initial period with IMG I didn't feel I was making much headway, and after about three years I told Mark I was going to leave.

He didn't argue with me, but shortly Bud Stanner, one of the IMG executives, came and met me in Hartford, Connecticut, and gave me a big spiel about how much they could do for me. I just listened, and said 'Yes, yes, yes' a few times; he went away, but I was still unconvinced. Six weeks later he came and saw me in Tucson, Arizona, and gave me an even bigger spiel. I finally agreed that I would re-sign, so he said:

'Terrific. If you just sign here then . . .' and pulled out a bunch of papers.

Slowly, though, I was learning. I said: 'I'll sign, but on one condition.'

'Oh,' he said, 'what's that?'

'On condition that your name goes on the contract and you'll be responsible for everything the company can do for me.'

That put his name on the line, linked to various named projects that we agreed to work on together. Since then, we've become good friends, formed a good working relationship, and I continue to earn good money from tennis despite the fact that I haven't played on the circuit for a number of years. We've had to work at it, of course, but the important thing is that we've worked at it together. With some players, I get the impression that they don't have sufficiently clear aims and this leads them to place too much faith in the agent. They sit back and wait for the contracts to roll in when they should be out there themselves, helping to show that they are the right kind of person for a particular promotion or endorsement. If player and agent don't work at the job together, the result usually is that both sides end up feeling let-down and frustrated.

Looking at agents today, and considering the money that's available in tennis, I feel it has become almost unbelievably tough for the young player coming up through the sport. As soon as a young player shows a certain degree of promise, the commercial approaches start to arrive. Perhaps the first offer the player receives is for a racket contract. This could well come before the player has even thought about getting an agent, maybe at the age of fifteen. From the company's point of view, this is fine: they don't want to deal with an agent, they'd much rather talk to the kid. I know of one kid who has signed a contract with a manufacturer for $25,000 a year to endorse clothing, rackets and shoes – when the contract is really worth $100,000 a year. So it's costing the kid

$75,000 a year to have signed without consulting people in the know, who could have helped him.

Eventually the player gets an agent. If he or she continues to show the same promise, some very attractive deals should come in. With someone of exceptional talent, this can soon reach the stage where the player knows in advance, before hitting a ball, that he or she has as much as $200,000 secure in the bank for that year. It then becomes difficult for that player to keep a cool head, and not make compromises with his original ideal of becoming the No 1 player in the world. He buys a sports car, starts enjoying the night life, his face and name appear in advertisements . . . in short, he becomes a celebrity, particularly in his own country. All this attention can easily detract from the quality of his tennis. A falling-off, say, of 10 per cent makes all the difference between becoming the top player in the world and settling instead for a good living and a place around No 20 in the ratings.

Another problem is over-eagerness. Imagine a player with good potential who has decided to sign with an agent. Having done so, he wants to see some money coming in. This puts pressure on the agent, who responds by arranging some exhibition matches for the player so that the accounts will look better. Let's say the player's future schedule requires him to play three weeks of tournament tennis, followed by a one-week break, followed by three more weeks of tennis. Now, instead of taking the week off and resting somewhere, doing some training, thinking about his game, taking videotapes of it and looking at them – instead of doing all these useful background jobs, plus having a rest from the tensions of matchplay, he has to go and play exhibition matches in the short-term cause of gathering a few extra bucks.

'Operation Tennis'

In Australia Tony Roche and I now run a junior development programme called 'Operation Tennis', and we are trying to devise some paths through the commercial minefield for the younger players. Our idea is for Operation Tennis to sign them up at around the age of fourteen or fifteen. This way, when the manufacturing companies and the agents start their mating calls, the players have to come back to us and get our agreement to any deal that has been proposed. We then take a small percentage of the agent's percentage, which we put back into our tennis

programme to help the future generations of young players.

    This system also allows us to keep a closer check on the young player and how he develops. Deals can be vetoed if we feel they will not help the player realize his full potential. If, after all, he gets to a financially comfortable position, such as I described earlier, then decides to sit back and enjoy life, not only will he never reach the top, but our time and Operation Tennis's time will have been largely wasted. Neither Tony nor I take a cent from the scheme, and we are mean about wasting our time. So the people we coach need to have the highest ideals and must be prepared to work very hard to achieve them. With us, the leading question is not 'Do you want a tax problem?' it's 'Do you want to be No 1 in the world?'

Hey, Tony,' I said, 'we'd better go out tonight. Have a few beers.'

Tony Roche had been living like a monk for close on two weeks and I was worried about him. It was not that his policy of self-deprivation had been a failure, rather the opposite. It was 1968 and he was enjoying an excellent Wimbledon. So far he had played in the singles final, losing to Laver; then he and I had won partial revenge the same day by defeating Emerson and Laver in four sets in the doubles semi-final. Now, on that Friday evening, we faced the prospect of a final next day against Fred Stolle and Ken Rosewall.

My own Wimbledon had been more convivial than Tony's. On the first Saturday I had been eliminated from the singles by Arthur Ashe, and I spent several evenings of the second week out on the town with Owen Davidson, whose flat in Putney Tony and I were sharing. This had proved an exhilarating substitute for singles play, and if Owen and I were less bright than Tony at the breakfast table, I had been in more-than-adequate shape on the afternoons when it mattered and we had played good doubles.

With one Wimbledon final lost, and one to play, Tony could have been forgiven for wanting one last quiet night in front of the television with his cup of cocoa. But after giving it some thought he agreed to come with me to a dinner in Knightsbridge. By 9.30 or so, he was beginning to look around him and come up with his own ideas. He suggested that we should drop in on the Russians. It was still early, too early to head back to the flat, so we set out for the Russian team's hotel.

Despite the solemnity of his Wimbledon fortnight compared with mine, Tony had been quietly sharing samovars lately with one of the Russian girls; he also knew that the Russians were having a party that evening to celebrate their interpreter's birthday.

We arrived at the hotel around 10.15 – but too late! All the players had gone to bed. In the foyer the only survivors were the interpreter, the

team manager and some other officials, plus the hotel owner and his wife. It wasn't a party exactly, but someone fetched two more glasses, and filled them with vodka. We emptied those and the bottle came round again. And again...

On our way to the Russians' hotel, I'd had it in mind to say hello to Sergei Likhachev. A huge player, built like a tank, he and I had drunk a few toasts on past occasions. Now, buoyed up by a few early-evening beers, the wine at dinner, and the recent sampling of the vodka, I was eager to renew the friendship. Someone gave me a room number and I rushed upstairs. I saw no need to knock, so charged into the room shouting:

'Where are you, Sergei, you bastard? I want you!'

The light went on. I wheeled round, looking for Sergei; instead, three pairs of eyes stared at me. I looked again and saw three Russian junior players wrestling for a logical explanation as to why John Newcombe should be standing in the middle of their bedroom, hollering abusive language at Sergei. Sergei? They were not called Sergei.

I made the most dignified exit I could, lobbing the juniors a couple of verbal rockets for being in the wrong room, and set off again in search of Likhachev. Eventually I got hold of him and he came downstairs. The Big Boss of the Russian team was not around at the time, so Sergei dived into the vodka and lit a cigarette. We chatted away, Sergei happily gulping and puffing with the rest – even though he was the only Russian player present.

The door swung open and in walked... the Big Boss! Straight away Sergei whisked his cigarette into his pocket – and held it there! I tried not to stare and give the game away when the Big Boss came over to talk to us. Sergei was quite impassive. He gave no sign of pain; no tell-tale smoke came from his pocket, so he must have extinguished the cigarette by squeezing it to death. When the boss left the room some while later, this was confirmed. The cigarette emerged, a smashed and crumpled corpse of yellow fibres and greyish paper, blackened at one end. Sergei grinned and threw it into a fire bucket: Russian stiff upper-lip at its most convincing.

Banana splits

Next thing, Tony and I had got involved in a banana-eating contest. Well, it was more or less the next thing we did. Probably one or two other things happened in between, which memory refuses to recall, because by this time we were upstairs in another part of the hotel. I was leaning out of a window trying to get rid of an overload of banana, and Sergei was lumbering across the room to see if he could help.

In most situations, I guess, Sergei could be relied on to think big. His solution to helping a man get rid of an excess of banana was typical: push the man *and* the banana through the window. That way, no more banana. So simple! Sergei grabbed me round the legs and hefted me into a horizontal firing position.

'What are you doing, you bastard?' I shouted. When it was all too clear what the Russian mammoth was trying to do, I began yelling for Tony and flailing about with my arms to try and get a grip on a piece of window-frame; at least it might gain some time, I figured, while it dawned on Tony that if he didn't do something – and quick – he would be minus a doubles partner at his next Wimbledon final. At last the full horror of finishing lone runner-up to Stolle and Rosewall (and having to explain the reason why) must have got through to him. He hurled himself like a goalkeeper at the window and pulled it down with a crash on my back. Then he gripped the base of the frame to keep me firmly jammed there while he thought what to do next.

Tony and Sergei were well-matched. Minutes passed and the vertical pressure of Roche was still in dynamic contention with the horizontal thrusts of Likhachev when, for the second time that evening, the door swung open and . . . in walked the Big Boss. Sergei's reaction was predictable. Even faster than he had buried the lighted cigarette in his pocket, he threw my legs to the floor and spun round to stand rigidly to attention before his superior. From my

HONESTLY! I'VE NEVER SEEN HIM BEFORE IN MY LIFE!

position, half overhanging the street, I grinned and nodded my appreciation through the window pane. It was the effective end of the party. Tony helped me back into the room and we made our way home to Putney.

The next day the match with Stolle and Rosewall was long and physically punishing. We went into the fourth set 2–1 down, and had to play twenty-six games to force our opponents into a decisive fifth set (no tie-breakers then). We took the last set 6–4, and collapsed in our chairs. Then, after towelling ourselves, we got up to receive the trophy. A few moments later, weary but happy, we walked over to the dressing-room.

We opened the door . . . and there was the entire Russian team! Tears of joy were on their faces. They cheered us, hugged us, kissed us, roared and wept with exultation. We loved it. This was great. But after a while we wondered if they weren't overdoing it a little, even for Russians. At last I managed to get an explanation from Alex Metreveli.

'For weeks we've been going to bed at ten o'clock,' he said. 'No outings. No fun. If we travel, we have to have extra sleep to make us fit. All the time, the bosses are strict. They see only one way of doing things. Then, this afternoon, we were all sitting together in the stand and you were losing two sets to one and we feared you would lose the match. The Big Boss turned to us and said: "You see! Staying out late. Not going to bed at proper time. You see what happens!"' Alex gave a huge beam of pleasure. 'And then you turned round and won the match. No wonder we are so happy!'

We see very little of our Russian friends these days. The reasons for this are political and go back to the period leading up to the Moscow Olympics of 1980. The Russian team was still playing the Western circuit, but problems were beginning to arise between the ITF, the world governing body of tennis, and the Russian Tennis Association. The argument was over the players' status as amateurs or professionals. On the one hand, the players were picking up prize money which, in the ITF view, confirmed that they were professionals. The fact that they were not allowed to keep the money, but had to pass it on to the Russian Association, was seen as immaterial by the world body.

The Russians, on the other hand, insisted that their players be regarded as amateurs on the grounds that they received no payment beyond their living expenses. These protestations failed also to conceal a crafty plan whereby the Russian players would shortly participate in the forthcoming Olympics and win everything. Although tennis was not an official sport, the commissars in Moscow evidently reckoned that the success of their players in a fringe tournament, given suitable publicity and television coverage, would be a profitable exercise in sporting propaganda.

It became inevitable that the Russians' inflexibility and blatant deviousness would get sufficiently far up the nose of the ITF for there to be a showdown. This happened, and the Russians were given an ultimatum: either declare that your players are professionals, in which case they can accept prize money, or declare that they are amateurs. As amateurs, they can still take part in the tournaments, but they will only be entitled to expense money. This in effect meant their air fare to the event from the last place they were playing at, plus their living expenses, then running at about $28.00 a day.

Back in Russia, the commissars did not like being ordered around. They got huffy and pulled their players out of the circuit. And that is why,

at the time of writing, you can see players competing in the West from all the other Eastern Bloc countries, but you won't find a single Russian.

The camera trade

Many years ago I had a fascinating two-week glimpse, from the inside, of Mother Russia and how the average citizen gets by despite all the rules and bureaucracy. With the Australian team I toured Moscow, Leningrad, Tallin and Riga. Each place we came to, people were sidling up to us at the courts and asking to meet us later, usually at our hotel. Either that, or they came straight to the hotel anyway.

In the West, it is normal for the tournament organizers and the Press to know where the players are staying; also there are always a few fans with inside information. In Russia, *everyone* seemed to know where the players could be found. The reason, I guess, is that only a few hotels in any Russian city are open to Western visitors, and the choice is easily narrowed for the average citizen going about his private enterprise.

From our point of view, as the steady stream of visitors came tapping on our bedroom doors, it seemed that the old days of the tennis bums must have been like this – days when a touring buccaneer would sell the shirt off his back to keep going (not to mention whatever he might have stashed away in the hollow handle of a racket).

There was an added complication. Money. Roubles were no good to us, since we couldn't take them with us. So what could we take? The answer, with grinding regularity, was: a camera. In the course of my two weeks in Russia the contents of my travelling bag saw some radical changes. Out went: five tennis shirts, six rackets, six pairs of sweatbands and half a dozen miscellaneous items. In came: various miscellaneous baubles . . . and eight Russian cameras.

'Great!' I thought to myself at the time. Back in Australia, however, I found that the market for foreign cameras was OK – provided you had a source of spare parts and accessories. But since it also appeared that the only trade route to Australia for Russian cameras was the one plied by tennis players, I had to conclude that my stock was totally worthless and ended up giving the whole lot away to a friend who collected cameras.

One particular incident from that sequence of hotel visits sticks in

my memory. Among the rackets I was prepared to barter was one with a flaw in it. Unless the client really knew about tennis rackets he probably would not notice the tiny crack just inside the top of the head. When the next client arrived, we went through the usual polite openers, then we fixed our deal. He took the flawed racket, and I added another Russian camera to my travelling bag. I made no mention to him of the crack in the racket, having persuaded myself that at least he had a racket he couldn't buy in Russia, and that he might be able to use it for several years – so long as he did not hit the ball too hard or play too often! A small cloud of guilt hung over the deal, but I put it out of my mind.

Next day I was at the tennis courts and an attendant came up to me in the dressing-room. There was someone outside who wished to see me. I followed him out, and was not overjoyed to find my visitor from the day before. What put me out was not that he was angry or waving a busted racket at me – which might well have been the case – but he now wanted to present me with a gigantic basket of fruit.

'My wife and I want you to have this,' he said simply, 'since you were so very kind yesterday.'

'Jesus,' I thought, and wanted to crawl into the ground. 'First I swindle the guy, then he comes back with presents.' When I had got over my initial confusion, I motioned to him to wait while I went back into the dressing-room. I found another racket – one of the last two I had with me – and took it out and gave it to him.

'Look,' I said, 'you have been so nice to me, I want you to have another racket.'

He was as thrilled as a small boy. He jumped about, clutched his hands together and gazed up at the heavens. Another racket! Only after many, many thank-yous and grateful bows did he finally draw back into the crowd – a truly happy Russian.

Looking back now on the incident, I wonder if that Russian and I are genuinely quits. I like to think that we are, even though I have to admit that I never did tell him about the crack in the racket. Some guilt lingers on my side. On the other hand, suppose he had slipped me a bum camera in the first place, and his wife had then shamed him into bringing round the fruit. Is that too mean or far-fetched? Probably. Also, it sounds more like something from a spy movie. *Real* Russians aren't like that. Are they . . .?

Joining up with World Team Tennis – that frenetic North American inter-city circuit of the mid-Seventies – had a remarkable effect on the nervous systems of some of the players. Because of the way the contests were organized, fifteen out of sixteen matches were played away from home in front of wild and hostile crowds. The fact that it was our own promoters who were largely responsible for encouraging those crowds to extend the boundaries of wildness and hostility, didn't altogether banish a feeling that somehow we'd been transported back through time to Ancient Rome.

The clamour, whistling and hollering rose up deafeningly on all sides of dressing-rooms from Honolulu to Philadelphia. Cross-eyed from lack of sleep, after weeks of touring, we'd pull on our fighting colours and step into the sunlight to meet the next version of that increasingly familiar combination: the golden home boy who could do no wrong, even though he may have been born in another continent, and the decidedly home-grown match-official, apparently yet another close relative of Emperor 'Thumbs Down' Nero.

If, as sporting comparisons go, you think that's a fraction over-dramatic, my answer is that, back in 1974 when I signed for World Team Tennis, I wouldn't have believed it either. At that time I was looking for one more year of serious competitive tennis before going on to develop one or two projects on the sidelines of the game. WTT seemed to fit my needs: a summer series of matches between players who each represented one of sixteen American cities. It seemed it could be fun. A lot of the women players were in favour, having successfully gone their own way earlier in the decade. I was the first male player to enlist. I signed for Houston (just down the road from my tennis ranch); a nation-wide circus was rapidly assembled, and the 'fun' began.

Looking back after even this brief interval, I find it hard to analyze precisely what it was that made World Team Tennis one of the most

gruelling circuits I have ever played. Partly it was the crowds who, from the start, were urged on by the promoters to root for 'their' adopted players, almost regardless of who was on the other side and what they might have felt about them at a more normal, open event. In a strange and disconcerting way, World Team Tennis exerted on spectators the nationalistic pull of Davis Cup matches, even though the contestants were the 'city-states' of basically one nation. From the spectators' point of view it wasn't very different, I guess, from cheering on your local football or baseball team. But for us tennis players it *was* different; and we didn't feel entirely comfortable with it.

The rules of Team Tennis (after a couple of weeks nobody except the organizers used the term 'World') were another disconcerting factor. To make the game 'more exciting', the rules of tennis as laid down by the ILTF were touched up more than somewhat. Matches consisted of five one-set contests – of men's and women's singles, men's and women's doubles, and mixed doubles – and deuce was replaced by 'no-ad scoring'. This meant that when players got to three points each, the winner of the next point won the game. It was all high-speed, quick-kill stuff (no chance of boring the customers with an old-fashioned finely balanced five-setter).

The same wham-bang urgency was injected into the players' schedules. Bug-eyed and bleary, we tracked across the States from Calgary to Houston to San Francisco to Pittsburg . . . Pittsburg was the home of the wildest spectators of them all. In my whole playing career I have only 'snapped' on two occasions; aptly enough, the first of these was in Pittsburg.

We had been on the road for two weeks of non-stop playing and travelling. I had a bad cold and felt very tired. Out on court, before the hooting burghers of Pittsburg, I was 4 – 4 against Ken Rosewall. We had reached three points each on my service, and by the rules of Team Tennis whoever won the next point would go 5 – 4 up. I hit a ball right through the line, and straight away Ken and I started to change ends. There was no argument between us; we both accepted I had won the point, and so did the linesman who called it good. Then the central umpire – the local man – overruled the linesman and called the ball out. I couldn't believe it; it was plain cheating by the 'home' official. Suddenly all my fatigue, aches, pains concentrated in an inner shriek of protest. Veins started to pop out on my head, and I charged at the umpire's chair.

I won't even try to remember the words I used, but most of them still can't be used on television. Just yelling, though, was not enough. I wanted the umpire himself, his heart, his guts, liver, anything I could get my hands on. I gripped his chair and started shaking it. The umpire started to rock sideways and his chair juddered precariously on its four stilt-like legs. There was alarm on his face, sure enough, but to the madman beneath this was not enough. I – wanted – him – OUT!

The Pittsburg crowd were lapping up the prospect of real gore at last – and on their own home court! Had they sought a more balanced view of what was being enacted, they could have looked down to one side of the court where three of the women players – Lesley Bowrey, Helen Gourlay and Karen Krantzcke – were in tears. They had all known me for years, and they knew well enough what had happened; they knew that this was tennis gone berserk. They also knew that, under the pressures we were playing to, it could easily happen again. And so it did.

The man who aced girls

We just about managed to shrug off the Pittsburg incident. My cold got better, even if my general feeling of tiredness did not. Later on that same trip, we were playing in a big indoor arena in San Francisco. I was in the mixed doubles, playing against Jimmy Connors and his partner. Connors and I were then Numbers One and Two in the world, and about six thousand people had come to watch. Mixed doubles has never been my favourite branch of tennis, and that evening, somehow, I kept acing the girl.

How to Shake an Umpire

To begin with, it was innocent enough. I served an ace, and there were one or two murmurs of 'Unfair', 'Acing the girl, huh?' – but nothing to get worried about. But as the game went on, the aces kept flowing and more and more people started picking it up. Soon enough it had spread right through the crowd, the murmurs turned to shouts and boos and the scene began to turn ugly. Towards the end of the set I'd had enough. Next serve, I threw up the ball and just cracked it as hard as I could. As soon as I hit it, I knew it was an ace. I followed through, then as the ball struck the back of the court I came up from the follow-through with the racket and jerked it in a great 'Up-yours' at that section of the crowd facing me. Then I went round the court and repeated the gesture until everyone in the crowd had received, at least once, the benefit of my feelings. There was uproar. If they'd been in two minds before, now they *all* knew they hated me.

We played out the set, and when it was over I stamped off the court, grabbed my rackets and went straight to the dressing-room. As I got to the dressing-room door I noticed two girls waiting outside. They stepped over, and very politely said:

'Mr Newcombe, can we please have your autograph? We . . .'

The rest of what they had to say was drowned out in a cascade of abusive language. When I'd ripped off this salvo, I crashed past them into the dressing-room and kicked the door emphatically shut. Once inside, I threw my rackets round the room then planted myself on a bench and sat there unmoving in a black and silent rage. The team trainer came in. He looked round at the fallen rackets, then after about five minutes, when he thought it was safe to start a conversation, he said:

'Hey, I feel sorry for those two poor girls out there. What did you say to them?'

I gave him a rough idea, and he said:

'Yeah. Thing is, John, they've driven down, I guess two hundred miles, just to watch you play. They must be two of your greatest fans.'

'Ah,——!'

It was still another ten minutes before I could bring myself to do it, but then I got myself off the bench and went out to look for the girls.

Luckily for me, they were still there. I brought them back into the dressing-room, apologized for the things I'd said and signed autographs for them. When they left, they seemed reasonably happy; at least there had been time to mend one or two broken fences.

So much, then, for Team Tennis. Too high-powered to last, it barely staggered into its second year – though without me, and without quite a few of its other founder-players, not to mention most of its original sponsors. It sputtered briefly again, then collapsed forever after the 1978 season. For me it did provide one or two happier moments (see 'The Calgary Burlesque', below) but on the whole it was not widely mourned.

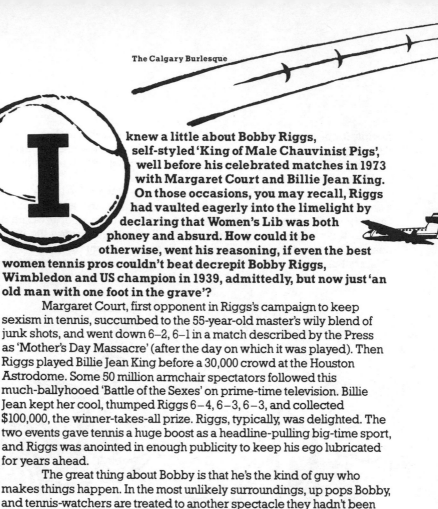

I knew a little about Bobby Riggs, self-styled 'King of Male Chauvinist Pigs', well before his celebrated matches in 1973 with Margaret Court and Billie Jean King. On those occasions, you may recall, Riggs had vaulted eagerly into the limelight by declaring that Women's Lib was both phoney and absurd. How could it be otherwise, went his reasoning, if even the best women tennis pros couldn't beat decrepit Bobby Riggs, Wimbledon and US champion in 1939, admittedly, but now just 'an old man with one foot in the grave'?

Margaret Court, first opponent in Riggs's campaign to keep sexism in tennis, succumbed to the 55-year-old master's wily blend of junk shots, and went down 6–2, 6–1 in a match described by the Press as 'Mother's Day Massacre' (after the day on which it was played). Then Riggs played Billie Jean King before a 30,000 crowd at the Houston Astrodome. Some 50 million armchair spectators followed this much-ballyhooed 'Battle of the Sexes' on prime-time television. Billie Jean kept her cool, thumped Riggs 6–4, 6–3, 6–3, and collected $100,000, the winner-takes-all prize. Riggs, typically, was delighted. The two events gave tennis a huge boost as a headline-pulling big-time sport, and Riggs was anointed in enough publicity to keep his ego lubricated for years ahead.

The great thing about Bobby is that he's the kind of guy who makes things happen. In the most unlikely surroundings, up pops Bobby, and tennis-watchers are treated to another spectacle they hadn't been expecting. He is always both entertaining and a fine sportsman – and, I should add, an enthusiastic gambler. This reputation goes back to pre-war times, when he backed himself to win the 1939 Wimbledon singles, doubles and mixed doubles – and did so.

Some while before

Riggs v The Women, I was due to play Andres Gimeno in a singles semi-final at Wimbledon. I got there at 12 o'clock in good time to change and warm up for the 2 o'clock start. There was no-one in the dressing-room when I arrived. That was okay, but as time went by and still no-one turned up I became more acutely aware that I hadn't arranged for anyone to hit with before the match. At 12.30 still no-one had come. Then Bobby Riggs walked in.

'Hey, Bobby,' I said, greatly relieved, 'would you come out and hit with me?'

'Sure, sure,' said Bobby. He got changed, we walked over to a back court and I went through my warm-up routine, which took about half an hour. All the time I was keeping an eye on the clock, and soon it was 1.10. I was keen to go back, shower, change and get myself ready for the 2 o'clock match. Then Bobby said:

'I tell you what, let's have a game.'

'Well, I don't think I can, Bobby. I have to go back, shower . . .'

'No, no.' Bobby brushed my worries aside. 'Not yet. We'll just have a quick game right now. We'll play two games. You play into the singles court and I'll play the doubles court. Let's make it £10 a game, huh?'

'But Bobby. I've got to go and play in this semi-. . .'

'No, no. No, no. We'll play one game, just one game. OK?'

By now quite a few people had gathered round the court and Bobby was beginning to act up to them. 'Come on, it'll loosen you up. I mean, just *one* game!'

In the end I bargained him down to two games (he'd never have been satisfied with one). In deference to his age he was allowed one alley, or tramline, and I had first serve only; also, I wasn't allowed to hit a winner. The stake remained at £10 a game.

I don't like to rush my tennis, but with less than forty minutes to go before I was due on court with Gimeno, it was pretty hard *not* to go for winners. Anyhow, I beat him, pocketed the £20 and rushed away to change for what I still considered was the main event of my day, and just about made it.

GGS NUDE, FREE-FALL INTO A PLATE OF STRAWBERRIES EVENT

The secret jockstrap

That was in 1970, and I didn't play Bobby again – although we ran into each other plenty of times on the circuit – until Calgary, in 1974. There I was playing in a Team Tennis match, and at half-time it was announced to the 3,000 spectators that John Newcombe and Bobby Riggs had agreed to play a special exhibition match of . . . *Strip Tennis*!

All my games with Bobby seem to require special rules. This time we played to a simple code whereby every time you lost a point, you had to remove an article of clothing. (Forewarned, I had loaded up in the dressing-room with a spare jockstrap, which I stuffed loose down the front of my shorts.)

We started to play and I took the first three points. In turn Bobby (also well-prepared) pulled off a sweater, then another sweater, then another sweater. I took the next point, and that cost him his shirt. Then he had to take off a shoe . . . and then *he* won a point!

I threw my racket down in disgust and embarrassment, walked this way and that, as though I was deeply troubled about which

LET GO! IT'S MINE!

piece of clothing I ought to take off. Then, after a suitably impressive interval, I stuck my hand deep down inside my shorts and started pulling, stretching and wriggling round the court. At last I managed to wrench out this spare jockstrap, which I threw in triumph high in the air.

There was wild applause. Then, on with the game. A few points later I had everything off Bobby except a tiny pair of briefs. It was my turn to serve. I came in and whacked the ball as hard as I could. As it shot past Bobby for a winner, the crowd roared their delight and I gave Bobby an encouraging gesture to help him remember what he had to do next. As it turned out, Bobby had no need of any explanation from me. He already knew what he had to do. He turned, dashed off court and shot inside the dressing-room – the fastest near-naked tennis player west of Medicine Hat!

I SAW IT FIRST!

Disgruntled players and newspaper reporters have been saying for years that Wimbledon is over the hill, over-rated, old-fashioned, uncomfortable, inconvenient, too far from the centre of London, too choked with traffic. Players say they can't find a decent practice court within three hours' drive (to listen to them, Eastbourne must be about the nearest). Reporters reveal to us each year that the strawberries are getting mushier and more expensive, the queues for the toilets are longer, the toilets when you get inside are more smelly than ever; even the rain is worse, it's harder, blacker, and gets down your neck quicker.

They can say what they like, they are ignoring the essential point. Wimbledon is the red-carpet event of tennis. It has the supreme tradition, and an atmosphere that is very special. It may be a bit stiff-upper-lip, but it's special. No other country can match it, and that's why Wimbledon is still held in such high regard by the great majority of people. Most players realize this, and they also realize that Wimbledon is a keystone in the international set-up which enables them to earn millions of dollars a year.

As for the way the tournament is organized, perhaps Wimbledon has not progressed in recent years as rapidly as some other major events – I'm thinking particularly of the French championships – but to claim it has not progressed, or that it has regressed, is patently wrong. Some of the little things could be better, and the appointment in 1982 of Ted Tinling as a kind of resident ambassador showed that the Committee was conscious of this, and prepared to work on it. In the dressing-room, meanwhile, *all* players – from No 1 to No 128 – are well looked after during the fortnight. They have a courtesy car to bring them to the court and take them back to where they are staying, and they share equal opportunities for using the practice courts, of which there are twenty-six, as well as free transport there and back. They also get their lunches free,

and their afternoon teas as well.

It may be that tennis and Wimbledon, like some other sports and sporting institutions, have been the victim of too much exposure in the press, and on radio and television. A good recent example has been the hysteria over the fact that Wimbledon has grass. Every year that it rains at Wimbledon, people blame the grass because there is no play. If there was a synthetic surface, they say, there wouldn't be so many interruptions. They forget that the courts are soon protected with covers when it rains, and that play has to stop on any outdoor court when it is too wet to continue. That is as true for the synthetic courts at Flushing Meadow, or the clay of the Stade Roland Garros, as it is for Wimbledon. As far as I'm concerned, grass-court play is one of the finer arts of tennis, and Wimbledon should keep its grass just as long as the groundstaff can make it grow there.

I'd really prefer one of those big ones you can dry yourself on
Back in the Sixties, some of the necessary comforts *were* in short supply at Wimbledon. Such as towels. It was all right if you were on the Centre Court or No 1 Court: then you were given a big green towel to take out on court with you. But if you were on an outside court, you were issued with a piece of cloth about one foot long and nine inches wide, more suited to drying teacups than to mopping up the sweat that accumulates in three and a half hours' matchplay.

After your match, though, whichever court you were playing on, you could have a bath-size towel for your bath or shower. Once we knew what to expect, we got round the official procedure by claiming we wanted a bath as soon as we'd arrived and changed. The big towel was rapidly transferred to a locker until it was time to play, then smuggled out to the court under a sweater.

The ritual of the towels is no longer part of the charms of Wimbledon. In fact, most rules and regulations can be changed if people go about it the right way. For players, that means getting on the board of the players' association and lobbying for what they want, not moaning to newspaper reporters who will write a piece that fits their designs and not the players'.

Back in 1969, Wimbledon only allowed a three-minute warm-up period. We had just formed our first players' association and we went to the Wimbledon Committee and presented our case for extending the warm-up. We had to argue with them, but we were determined and pointed out that three minutes didn't allow the players enough time to hit their ground shots, then some volleys and smashes, then some serves. There was also the fact that warm-ups were only effective if the player really did warm up – and wasn't then liable to pull a muscle in the opening minutes. It was a long argument, but we got the period extended to four minutes, which was regarded as a major coup. Now players get five minutes, but that revised arrangement was only made after further discussion and careful negotiation.

Another coup for us was to get a short warm-up period inserted after a break in play. As matters then stood, you had to come back after a break for rain and immediately restart the match. Now you can have one minute to get your system circulating properly before you resume play.

Horizontal hitchhiker

Occasionally, even at Wimbledon, things go wrong not because of some strange or out-of-date regulation but simply because Fate steps in to engineer a piece of chaos that no-one could be blamed for failing to foresee.

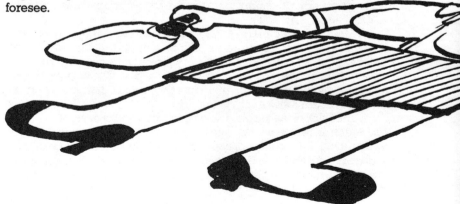

At the 1982 championships the progress of Jo Anne Russell to the
ladies' quarter-finals was very nearly snuffed out before the third round
by a whole chain of transport disasters, enough to suggest to her that it
must be easier to travel to London from her native Miami than to reach
Wimbledon from her London hotel.

As she waited in the lobby of her hotel on the morning of her
third-round match with Pam Casale, it seemed as though the car she had
arranged to pick her up would never come. She was right, it never did.
After yet another look at the time, Jo Anne decided to strike out
for Wimbledon on her own . . . then found that she couldn't get a taxi.
Only slightly deterred, she pulled out a thumb and
started hitch-hiking. A kindly motorist stopped,
she explained her problem, and they set off

at last for Wimbledon. But Fate had not finished with Jo Anne Russell. Her rescue vehicle caught fire and had to be abandoned. She set off again, but by then the only people going in the direction of Wimbledon were late already for the tennis and had no eyes for the girl at the roadside waving a sports bag.

As more and more precious time slipped by, Jo Anne chose to abandon the sidelines and go for a winner. When the next car approached, she stepped off the pavement and lay down in the road in front of it. Although the British don't as a whole respond warmly to such blackmail tactics, eventually Jo Anne found a driver who didn't swerve narrowly past her on two wheels, but stopped and picked her up. She arrived at Wimbledon one hour forty minutes late for her match. Certain she had been disqualified, she approached an official who told her not to worry, her match had been postponed because of the rain. There is no available record of what Jo Anne said next.